THE

CASE

FOR

IMPEACHING

TRUMP

THE
CASE
FOR
IMPEACHING
TRUMP

ELIZABETH
HOLTZMAN

HOT BOOKS

Hot Books may be purchased in bulk at special discounts for sales promotion, corporate gifts, fund-raising, or educational purposes. Special editions can also be created to specifications. For details, contact the Special Sales Department, Skyhorse Publishing, 307 West 36th Street, 11th Floor, New York, NY 10018 or info@skyhorsepublishing.com.

Hot Books® and Skyhorse Publishing® are registered trademarks of Skyhorse Publishing, Inc.®, a Delaware corporation.

Visit our website at www.skyhorsepublishing.com.

10 9 8 7 6 5 4 3 2 1

Library of Congress Cataloging-in-Publication Data is available on file.

ISBN: 978-1-5107-4477-6

Cover design by Brian Peterson

Printed in the United States of America

Dedication

To Rebecca J. Folkman (1942–2017),
friend extraordinare, from the fourth grade—and always

Acknowledgements

This book could not have been written without the hard work, exceptional intelligence, scholarship, and dedication of Victoria Bassetti. I am deeply in her debt. Thanks, too, go to Marshall Sonenshine, investment banker, lawyer, documentary film producer, and now literary agent, for making this book happen, and for his faith in me. I want to salute Common Cause, Karen Hobert Flynn, its president, and Stephen Spaulding, its Chief of Strategy, for first suggesting that I think seriously and systematically about impeachment, and for generously supporting my effort. I am grateful to my publisher, Tony Lyons, my editor, Michael Campbell, and my copy editor, Janet Byrne, for taking on this project. My friend Judith S. Ames and my brother Dr. Robert N. Holtzman were wonderful cheerleaders throughout. I am especially thankful to my friend, Jayme B. Hannay, for her unflagging encouragement and patience. Any mistakes in the book are my own.

Contents

THE
CASE
FOR
IMPEACHING
TRUMP

1

Impeachment

When Donald Trump's presidential election victory was announced in the early morning hours of November 9, 2016, like many Americans, I rubbed my eyes in disbelief and dismay. Two questions raced through my mind:

What had become of America that a man so unfit, so small-minded, so mean-spirited could be elected? A man whose ethnic and racial bigotry had set the stage for his presidential run when he called Mexicans rapists and made racist birther attacks on President Barack Obama. Whose vulgarity and misogyny were laid bare in the *Access Hollywood* tape when he bragged about forcibly grabbing women by their genitals. Whose performance at presidential debates showed him not only flagrantly ill-informed, but manifestly unwilling to get informed.

My second question was how much harm this man would do to America as its 45th president.

I have my answer now to the latter, less than two years after the election. President Trump has damaged American democracy far more than I would have guessed. He has refused to protect our system of free elections from foreign interference; he has relentlessly attacked the administration of justice, in particular the investigation into a possible conspiracy with Russia regarding the 2016 presidential election, putting himself above the rule of law; he has failed to separate his personal business from the country's, flouting the Constitution's requirements; and he has violated the constitutional rights of the people in separating children from parents at the Southwest border without due process of law—and to cover up these misdeeds, he has systematically lied and assailed the press. These are "great and dangerous offenses" that the framers of our Constitution wanted to counteract and thwart. They provided a powerful remedy. Impeachment.

Many tremble at the word, fearing how President Trump's supporters will react to an impeachment inquiry, worrying that it will only further polarize an already deeply divided nation or that there will not be enough votes in the Senate to convict him even if the House of Representatives votes to impeach. Just calling for an inquiry will be viewed as a Democratic Party attack on the head of another party, a kind of coup d'état. It's easy to find reasons to be anxious.

I'm not afraid. As a junior congresswoman, the youngest ever elected at that time, I served on the House Judiciary Committee that voted to impeach President Richard Nixon for the high crimes and misdemeanors he committed in connection with the Watergate cover-up and other matters. Thorough, fair, and above all bipartisan, the committee acted on solid evidence presented in televised hearings that riveted the nation, handing us the blueprint for how impeachment can be successfully pursued today. In our 225 years of constitutional democracy, the Nixon impeachment process has proven to be the only presidential effort that worked. Though Nixon resigned—the only president ever to do so—two weeks after the committee's impeachment vote, he did so to avoid the certainty of being impeached and removed from office. We became a better nation for having held the president accountable.

All of which raises two further questions: Should we be considering the impeachment of President Donald J. Trump? Will we again become a better nation by pursuing that option? To answer, we need to set aside President Trump's unremitting attacks on the environment, on our close allies, on almost every program that President Obama put into effect, including the Affordable Care Act, and any disagreements we have over policy, as well as any personal animus, and ascertain simply whether he has engaged in the kind of egregious conduct that would meet the constitutional standards for impeachment and removal from office.

This means we have to focus sharply on his potentially impeachable offenses. In so doing, we will find it useful to compare them, when possible, to similar offenses by President Nixon found to be impeachable by the House Judiciary Committee in 1974. Here is a list of some of President Trump's potentially impeachable offenses developed as of this writing:

A possible interference with or obstruction of the administration of justice and an abuse of power. On May 9, 2017, Trump fired FBI Director James Comey, who was investigating both his national security adviser, Michael Flynn, and Russia's connections to the Trump campaign in connection with influencing the 2016 presidential election. Two days later, President Trump admitted to NBC's Lester Holt that Comey's firing had to do with "the Russia thing"—in other words, President Trump acknowledged that he was trying to shut down the FBI investigation into his possible conspiracy with Russia. (Flynn has since pleaded guilty to lying to the FBI.)

The Comey firing uncannily echoes Nixon's firing of the special Watergate prosecutor for seeking highly damaging information about the president—a brazen defiance of the rule of law that triggered the start of impeachment proceedings against Nixon.

A second possible interference with or obstruction of the administration of justice and an abuse of power. President Trump has persistently and publicly attacked those heading the Russia investigation, including special counsel Robert S. Mueller III and Deputy Attorney General Rod Rosenstein, and has repeatedly condemned Attorney General Jeff Sessions for recusing himself, suggesting that he wants to fire any and all of them in order to get control of the Russia investigation. (He actually did give an order to fire Mueller.)

A failure to take care that the laws are faithfully executed, as required by the Constitution. To try to deflect public concern about his possible role in conspiring with Russia about the 2016 election and to undermine the legitimacy of the investigation into that matter, President Trump has persistently attacked the Russia investigation as a witch hunt and a hoax, even though thirty-four people either pleaded guilty or were indicted as a result of that investigation. The indictments included Russian agents who allegedly interfered with the 2016 election by manipulating social media, hacking into computers of the Democratic National Committee (DNC), tampering with election machinery in various states, and using other methods.

Similar behavior by President Nixon became one of the grounds of the first article of impeachment against him. As part of the Watergate cover-up, Nixon was charged with making "false or misleading public statements for the purpose of deceiving the people of the United States." This included Nixon's claim that White House investigations had cleared everyone of any involvement with the break-in, for example, and that his aide H. R. Haldeman, who had perjured himself before the Senate Watergate Committee, had testified accurately.

A second failure to take care that the laws are faithfully executed, as required by the Constitution. President Trump has refused to undertake his constitutionally mandated leadership role to protect the 2018 midterm elections from further interference by the Russian government, despite the paramount importance of ensuring honest elections in our democracy. In the absence of that protection, the Russians may renew the cyberattacks and other interference used against us in the 2016 election.

An abuse of power. He has used the power of his office to remove or threaten to remove the security clearances of people who criticized him or who he believed were associated with the Russia investigation or could be possible witnesses against him. A historical equivalent is President Nixon's creation of an "Enemies List" of anti–Vietnam War activists, whom he directed to be audited by the Internal Revenue Service (IRS) in retaliation for their political positions—actions that formed part of an article of impeachment.

A second abuse of power. He approved a lawless, ethnically based, and infinitely cruel policy of separating children from parents at the Southwest border, depriving both children and parents of their constitutional rights and subjecting them to horrific mental anguish that may result in long-term psychological damage, a policy that the courts struck down.

An assault on our democratic values. He has systematically lied to the American people about government policies and actions, crippling their ability to make sound judgments about the direction of their government.

A violation of a specific constitutional prohibition. He has refused to separate himself from his business interests, which have received things of value from foreign and US governments, ranging from Chinese trademarks to payments for the use of his Washington hotel, suggesting that the presidency is open for business and that his personal business interests may influence his governmental decisions—all apparent violations of the emoluments clauses of the Constitution and possibly the ban on bribery as well. Though the House Judiciary Committee voted against an Article of Impeachment involving Nixon's receipt of emoluments from the federal government, notably in the form of improvements to his California and Florida properties, President Trump's business interests are far greater than Nixon's, and President Trump could have tried to cure the problem of foreign emoluments by getting congressional approval, which he has steadfastly refused to do.

An effort to undermine a core democratic institution. He has repeatedly attacked the media as the enemy of the people (a term used in the Stalinist purges against untold thousands of innocent people ultimately killed by the Soviet regime), encouraging Americans to disregard what they see and hear in the press as "fake news." Seriously undermining the free press hampers the public's right to know, which in itself hurts a democracy.

Nixon also attacked the press. He illegally ordered the wiretapping of journalists and placed a number of them on his Enemies List, targeting them for harassing IRS audits. Both actions formed a basis for Nixon's impeachment.

Actually, the catalog of President Trump's misdeeds goes on and on. The harm he has caused our democracy is great, and his misdeeds continue unabated. Resemblances to the impeachable conduct of Nixon persist. I have therefore come to the conclusion that an impeachment inquiry is not only justified under the Constitution of the United States, but imperative. In serving on the House Judiciary Committee during the Nixon proceedings, I acquired a niche expertise in impeachment that is, thankfully, not often needed. It is very much needed now, and I want to share it in this book.

IMPEACHMENT—A PERSONAL PERSPECTIVE

Forty-five years ago, impeachment wasn't a word that resonated with most Americans, including me. It burrowed its way into the national consciousness, however, after President Nixon began his second term of office and the Watergate cover-up broke apart. For weeks in the spring of 1973, Americans were glued to their television sets as a succession of Nixon appointees appeared before the Senate committee investigating the break-in and subsequent cover-up, variously perjuring themselves or chronicling the details of what happened. When a special prosecutor was appointed to conduct a serious investigation and then Nixon fired him, the nation demanded action from Congress, and I then lived with the realities of impeachment daily for more than nine months.

On June 17, 1972, five burglars broke into the Democratic National Committee headquarters at the Watergate complex in Washington, DC, attempting to plant bugs there. But a twenty-four-year-old security guard, Frank Wills, noticed something amiss in the building—adhesive tape that shouldn't have been there, covering locks—and called the police at 1:47 a.m. The burglars were arrested, and an address book belonging to one of them, Bernard Barker, revealed something unexpected: the name of E. Howard Hunt, a former CIA operative working in the Nixon White House. The president was then in the final months of his run for reelection against Senator George McGovern.

Keeping the connection to the break-in far, far from the president, his top aides and campaign officials became essential. Nixon was sure the break-in would prove little or no problem, as was made clear when the secret tapes of his Oval Office conversations were later made public. He claimed of the break-in: "Nothing loses an election. . . . [T]his damn thing now—it's going to be forgotten. . . . Who the hell's going to keep it alive?"

President Nixon was right about the election—his popular vote margin of victory over Senator McGovern remains the largest in American presidential history—but he was way off base about "this damn thing." Watergate wasn't forgotten, and in less than two years, he would resign his office in disgrace because of it.

The Watergate break-in made almost no impression on me at the time, even though my own campaign office in Brooklyn, New York, had been broken into by thugs around the same time and my campaign manager and another worker were beaten up, although luckily they didn't sustain any serious injuries. My opponent in the Democratic primary, the incumbent Emanuel Celler, had occupied that congressional seat for just shy of a half century, serving roughly half that time as chair of the House Judiciary Committee. Celler vastly underestimated me, likening me to a "toothpick trying to topple the Washington Monument." I won the primary, by a hair, and then the congressional seat—at thirty-one becoming the youngest woman ever to serve in Congress, a record I held for the next forty-two years. I had run on an anti-Vietnam War platform, defeating the powerful Brooklyn Democratic machine on a shoestring budget, and I swore to my constituents I would "stand up to the establishment," whether Democrats or Republicans.

I certainly had no inkling, in defeating Celler, of the form that standing up would take. Certainly, when the time came to ask for committee assignments, I made no attempt to take a seat on the Judiciary Committee, wanting to strike out in a different direction from the one my predecessor had taken. But the House leaders had other ideas. They put me on the Judiciary Committee, and I was not pleased, to put it mildly. This was a sign of how effective the cover-up had been. At that time, there seemed no possibility of impeachment proceedings against Nixon. If there had been, I would never have gotten such a plum assignment.

If only to help envision how such proceedings might materialize against President Trump, it's worthwhile to look back at how the tide turned against Nixon. As it has been said, "History doesn't repeat itself, but it often rhymes."

Of the key events that led to uncovering the White House connection to the Watergate break-in, the first came at the hands not of some Democratic fire-brand, but a conservative Republican judge, John J. Sirica. Presiding at the trial of the Watergate burglars, Sirica smelled a rat and concluded that higher-ups may well have been involved in the break-in. When he publicly suggested that possibility, in February 1973, James McCord, a former US intelligence officer who was part of the Watergate burglary team, wrote a letter to Sirica, which was made public in mid-March. McCord highlighted that political pressure had been applied to the defendants, leading to perjury and the omission of the names of higher-ups involved.

The second key event was the resignation, in the spring of 1973, of Attorney General Richard Kleindienst, who would later plead guilty to a criminal charge in connection with false testimony to the Senate. His resig-nation created an opening for a new attorney general, and when Nixon named Elliot Richardson to fill the position, the Senate Judiciary Committee saw an opportunity to mandate a serious criminal investigation into Watergate. The committee announced that it would not confirm Richardson unless he appointed a fully independent special prosecutor. Richardson agreed, and in May 1973, Archibald Cox, a Harvard Law School professor and former solic-itor general, became special Watergate prosecutor. The special Watergate prosecutor's office played a vital role in the Nixon impeachment by providing to the House Judiciary Committee, with court approval, a road map of factual evidence it had obtained during its investigation.

In this, it prefigured the report independent counsel Kenneth Starr sent to Congress on his investigation of President Bill Clinton's relationship with an intern, Monica Lewinsky, recommending his impeachment. Special counsel Mueller's role in impeachment remains to be seen.

When President Nixon ordered Cox's firing—to stop him from getting key tape recordings of White House conversations—it engendered such a public uproar that the House of Representatives was compelled to initiate an impeachment inquiry in response, ultimately leading to Nixon's resignation.

The third signal factor in bringing about President Nixon's downfall was the Senate's decision, in February 1973, to create a select committee to inves-tigate Watergate. Chaired by Senator Sam Ervin, a highly respected Democrat from North Carolina, the Senate Watergate Committee held extensive hear-ings. Ervin called himself a "country lawyer," a self-deprecating moniker that could not conceal his sagacity and constitutional law expertise. The Republican vice chair, Senator Howard Baker of Tennessee, started off as a strong Nixon partisan. Famously, he repeatedly asked, "What did the president know and when did he know it?"—thinking that the answers from witnesses would show that Nixon knew nothing and wasn't involved. When the answers showed otherwise, Baker bowed to reality and supported a thorough inquiry that would lead to the truth.

The star witness at the televised Senate Watergate hearings was John Dean, the White House counsel who had been fired before his appearance. Dean testified that he had been involved in the Watergate cover-up from early on. The most dramatic moment occurred when he swore that on March 21, 1973, he told President Richard Nixon in the Oval Office of a "cancer on the presidency"—of presidential pardons offered to the Watergate burglars and hush money paid to them. According to Dean, President Nixon said that he knew where and how to get more hush money. Of course, the president vehemently denied Dean's version of the conversation.

When the existence of a White House taping system became known in the summer of 1973, its significance was unmistakable. The substance of the March 21 conversation between Dean and President Nixon was no longer a "he said, he said" proposition. The tapes would resolve who was telling the truth, and the stakes couldn't have been higher: either Dean was lying or the president of the United States was involved in the cover-up of a burglary of DNC headquarters designed to interfere with the 1972 presidential election.

When the special Watergate prosecutor subpoenaed the Oval Office tapes, President Nixon suggested providing summaries. Cox rejected that suggestion. Then, on October 20, 1973, with a federal appeals court order that required the tapes be produced staring him in the face, the president ordered Cox fired. That, President Nixon must have thought, would put an end to the tapes controversy. But Attorney General Richardson refused to fire Cox—he had given his word to the Senate that Cox would be independent—and he resigned. Deputy Attorney General William Ruckelshaus also refused to follow the order and resigned. The third in line at the Justice Department, Solicitor General Robert Bork, was sworn in as the acting attorney general and, following the president's order, fired Cox.

These events became known as the Saturday Night Massacre—and it proved to be a watershed moment. The country was up in arms. Something was seriously wrong if the attorney general and his deputy, both Republicans, were resigning, and if President Nixon was fighting to stop the disclosure of tapes that theoretically could have proven him innocent. The American people demanded action from Congress, and numerous resolutions of impeachment were introduced in the House.

When the House impeachment inquiry began shortly thereafter, my work was cut out for me. I had to become fully acquainted with the business of impeachment, and while undertaking that huge assignment, I also had to attend to regular congressional business, still new to me. There was an agriculture bill (a particular conundrum for a city girl like me), a public works bill, and all the rest of the legislative agenda to digest and vote on, not to mention working to fulfill the promise I had made to my constituents to help end the Vietnam War. I had also become a plaintiff in a Brooklyn lawsuit with four bomber pilots to stop the US government's bombing of Cambodia without congressional approval. There was a lot to master all at once.

It took some time for the House Judiciary Committee to get organized, but it got there. John Doar, a Republican and former high-level Justice Department official, was appointed by the committee's Democratic majority as the committee's impeachment counsel, and the Republicans appointed their counsel, a Republican as well. This sent an important message—the Democrats on the committee were going to act in as bipartisan a manner as possible. The new committee chair, Peter Rodino of New Jersey, occupying his position thanks to my defeat of Celler, the former chair, in the primary, was mild-mannered and soft-spoken but very experienced in the ways of Washington. He understood that the country would never stand for having a partisan Democratic congressional majority remove a Republican president, particularly one elected in a landslide. It would be a naked display of power and seem blatantly undemocratic.

My first order of business was to comprehend fully the meaning of the Constitution's impeachment clause, something that was given no attention in law school. Impeachment, I learned, was meted out solely for presidential conduct that constituted "treason, bribery or other high crimes and misdemeanors." Treason was defined in the Constitution, and bribery seemed reasonably clear. Neither seemed to be involved in Nixon's misconduct. But the exact meaning of "high crimes and misdemeanors" was far trickier, and any impeachment proceedings against Nixon would have to focus on the phrase. We received a lengthy memo from the committee staff on "high crimes and misdemeanors," cowritten by then-staff member Hillary Rodham, but I wanted to know more. That sent me back to dry tomes about English legal history—a subject of no interest to me in law school—which is where impeachment precedents are found.

After studying the constitutional standard for impeachment, we had to deal with the facts of President Nixon's conduct. The amount of factual material committee members had to process and absorb was so overwhelming that I often felt as if I were sinking in quicksand. The committee staff compiled big, black three-ring binders that contained statements of facts and backup information. The staff then read the statements aloud to the committee members behind closed doors, where each one of us could question or dispute the statements. We had to lock the books every night in our own office safes. The wisdom of this approach was clear: no committee members could complain they didn't know what was going on or that they had not had an opportunity to object.

The statements of fact laid out what seemed to me to be an unending list of presidential wrongdoing and instances of abuse. We examined the intricacies of the Nixon campaign's plans for the Watergate break-in and the other schemes to disrupt the November election through so-called dirty tricks, such as the use of prostitutes to compromise Democratic delegates at their convention in Miami. Then we focused on the many layers of the cover-up. The cast of characters was large, ranging from former attorney general John Mitchell, who had approved the break-in and was part of the cover-up, to lower-level campaign officials, and from the president down to high and low White House officials. It even included the head of the Justice Department's criminal division, whom President Nixon pumped for information about the Watergate investigation, only to turn the information over to his top aides to help them avoid criminal liability.

The cover-up also involved misusing the CIA to stop the FBI's investigation, misusing the FBI by getting the director to deep-six incriminating material, blocking a potential congressional investigation into Watergate before the election, encouraging perjury by President Nixon's top aides, dangling offers of presidential pardons, and making the payments of hush money to keep the burglars quiet. All these items became part of the first article of impeachment (the cover-up article).

Another matter that found its way into Article I was President Nixon's "false or misleading public statements for the purpose of deceiving the people of the United State." For example, he publicly claimed that White House investigations cleared everyone of any involvement with the break-in. Another example occurred after his aide H. R. Haldeman testified falsely before the Senate Watergate Committee about Nixon's March 21 conversation with John Dean. President Nixon made a public statement saying that

Haldeman's false testimony was accurate. The cover-up would also be treated as an abuse of power in the second article of impeachment.

But there was more, much more, than the break-in and cover-up. Having approved illegal wiretaps of journalists and White House staffers, President Nixon hid the tapes in the White House. One of the staffers went to work for a Democratic presidential candidate, Senator Ed Muskie of Maine, giving Nixon a handy secret pipeline into the Muskie campaign. In addition to ordering IRS audits of political foes on his Enemies List—mostly people who opposed the Vietnam War—he established a special unit, the "Plumbers," that broke into the office of the psychiatrist of Daniel Ellsberg. Ellsberg was a military analyst who had leaked to the *New York Times* and the *Washington Post* a highly classified Defense Department study of US military and political involvement in Vietnam from 1945 to 1967, which came to be known as the Pentagon Papers. The burglars were looking for material with which to smear Ellsberg. President Nixon had also approved the Houston Plan, a blatantly illegal program to break into the homes and open the mail of antiwar activists and other "radicals" without court orders. The plan was allegedly withdrawn, but how much of it had been put into place? These matters would eventually be included in the second article of impeachment.

The list of other issues to examine included President Nixon's questionable tax write-off of about $500,000 for the donation of his papers to the National Archives, for which he used a backdated document, and whether US government improvements made to his California and Florida properties violated the emoluments clause of the Constitution. (An article of impeachment on taxes and emoluments was rejected by the committee.)

Of particular importance to me was President Nixon's secret bombing of Cambodia. Congress had banned any bombing of that country, but Nixon, paying no attention to the law, kept two sets of books about the bombing to allow him to violate the law with impunity. The fake set showed no bombing in Cambodia and was given to Congress to keep the fact of the bombing hidden. The other set of books showed the actual bombing sites. That was not given to Congress. Because it drastically undercut Congress's role in warmaking decisions, this deception prompted me to draft an article of impeachment on these grounds. (Although introduced, the article was not accepted.)

There are several things worth noting at this point. The impeachment effort did not start with a call for it by a special prosecutor, as happened in the failed President Clinton impeachment. There was, rather, a public outcry for congressional action. Though the Democrats then controlled the House of Representatives (and the Senate), there was no will on the part of the House leadership to take on impeachment until the Saturday Night Massacre, when our phones and mailboxes were flooded with messages from people all over the country.

The reluctance surprised me at the time. Some of us, including me, were getting a bit impatient with the inaction, particularly in light of the revelations produced by the Senate Watergate Committee and the president's continued efforts to expand his executive authority. But the hesitancy of the House leadership was also understandable in hindsight. Before Watergate, the only previous presidential impeachment was the failed effort to impeach President Andrew Johnson in the 1860s. Could Congress be trusted not to make the same mistake again? The House Judiciary Committee had a brand-new, untested chair and a large number of new members. Would they know how to handle this extremely explosive but delicate task? President Nixon had won in a landslide less than a year before. How would those who voted for him react to an impeachment—would the focus shift from the acts of the president to the acts of the committee? President Nixon posed a danger to the country, but impeachment posed a risk to the Democrats—or so it may have seemed at the time.

Ultimately, in July 1974, a little more than two years after the Watergate break-in and after an exhaustive—and exhausting—analysis of the law and the facts, the Judiciary Committee scheduled televised public hearings on whether to impeach President Nixon. During the debate on the articles of impeachment, Americans heard the committee members sincerely and thoughtfully grappling with the issues. There was very little grandstanding. Barbara Jordan, a new Democratic member from Texas, electrified everyone when she spoke about how the Constitution excluded her and other African Americans as full human beings with equal rights. I spoke of how I had listened carefully to White House tapes the committee received, waiting for the president to ask what was the right thing to do or what was in the public interest. He never did. When I later became district attorney in Brooklyn, the wiretaps of mobsters that I had to review seemed awfully familiar.

Under the Constitution, impeachments begin in the House of Representatives. If the House approves articles of impeachment by a majority vote, then there is a trial in the Senate, which must convict by a two-thirds vote. For the vote on the first article of impeachment, dealing with the cover-up in all its manifestations, six Republicans (roughly a third of the total) joined the yea votes of all the Democrats, which included three southerners from very pro-Nixon districts, for a tally of 27 to 11. An additional Republican joined the pro-impeachment vote on the second article of impeachment, dealing with President Nixon's various abuses of power, including those pertaining to the Watergate cover-up, for a tally of 28 to 10. The third article focused on Nixon's defiance of the impeachment process by refusing to respond fully to Judiciary Committee subpoenas for documents and for the tapes of forty-two White House conversations, thereby impeding the impeachment inquiry. It received the smallest number of votes, 21 to 17. (A copy of the President Nixon impeachment articles is contained in Appendix II.) The three articles, approved respectively on July, 28, 29, and 30, 1974, were sent to the House of Representatives for a vote on impeachment. Nixon resigned nine days later, before the full House could schedule a vote.

HOW OUR DEMOCRACY DEALT WITH WATERGATE: A BLUEPRINT FOR OUR TIMES?

The impeachment proceedings against Richard Nixon have withstood the test of time. In the forty-five years since the committee started its work in October 1973, no responsible attacks have been lodged against the fairness of the process or the correctness of the result—both of which were actually obvious at the time. That is why Richard Nixon became the only president ever to resign.

At the same time the impeachment votes were taken, in a case titled *United States v. Richard Nixon*, the Supreme Court ordered President Nixon to release certain tapes to special Watergate prosecutor Leon Jaworski, Archibald Cox's successor. Among them was the so-called smoking-gun tape, a recording of President Nixon's ordering his top aide, Haldeman, to direct the CIA to stop the FBI's investigation into Watergate using a false national security pretext. The tape irrefutably showed that the president was orchestrating the cover-up from the start. When the tape was made public, all of the holdout Republicans on the Judiciary Committee announced their support of impeachment.

With a now-unanimous pro-impeachment stance by all the Judiciary Committee members, and with almost universal praise for how the committee had conducted itself during the proceedings, it was clear that an overwhelming majority of House members would support impeachment and that the Senate would convict by two-thirds, if not more. There could be no legitimate opposition to President Nixon's removal from office for egregious wrongdoing. The president saw the proverbial handwriting on the wall and left office by resigning instead of suffering the humiliation of being forced out.

At the time, I believed that Watergate would stand as a stark warning to all future presidents, but that was not to be. The misdeeds of President Donald Trump have resurrected the word "impeachment," giving it new currency and life. Fierce emotions about the president have roiled the country. Charges and countercharges fly back and forth, including the explosive word *treason*.

Almost from the moment Donald Trump was elected, people have called for his impeachment. While premature, these calls reflected a deep discomfort with his presidency as well as a more than occasional misunderstanding of the impeachment process. Since the election, I have been asked numerous times to weigh in on the subject, to explain how impeachment works, and to draw parallels between what happened during the Nixon impeachment and what is happening now. Sadly, there are many similarities. As I did in 1973 and 1974, during Watergate, I am sorting through the facts (and yes, there *are* facts; this is not an alternative reality) and the law to try to give some clarity to impeachment and how it works.

For some, impeachment is something toxic to be avoided at all costs. Reining in presidential misconduct can be achieved other ways, they assert. But I see impeachment as the grand and solemn tool that our Founders gave us to address whether a president should be removed from office. When the time is right, they meant for us to use the tool. It was designed to protect our democracy and to preserve the rule of law. I believed the time was right in 1974, and I believe the time is right once again.

Watergate showed that despite President Nixon's reprehensible conduct, the rest of the system worked and could function as a real check on a rogue president. The courts worked. Republican judges, at the district court level and up to the Supreme Court and including every one of President Nixon's own appointees, put aside party for country and the rule of law,

Congress worked. The Senate Watergate Committee uncovered key facts about President Nixon's misconduct, and the Senate Judiciary Committee forced the appointment of the special Watergate prosecutor. The House Judiciary Committee voted on a bipartisan basis to hold the president accountable. The press worked. Led by two *Washington Post* cub reporters, probably too young to realize what it meant to take on a president, it was bold in searching out the facts and relentless in reporting them.

Will this happen again if we grapple with the Trump presidency? Will the other checks fall into place, including the courts and the Congress? Will the right-wing press, a mouthpiece for President Trump, find its footing on the truth? Will the bulk of the American people still put country over party and person? The answers to these questions are unknown, but they may be the key to whether America retains its vibrant democracy.

A fair, lawful, bipartisan impeachment inquiry into President Trump involves analyzing, with a clear head and heart, what he has done and what the Constitution requires. It means agreeing that we do not know where it will take us and that we do not know what the votes will be, agreeing to seek and accept the truth no matter what it turns out to be, whether it exonerates or inculpates the president. When we started the impeachment inquiry against President Nixon, nobody knew at the outset whether we had the votes in the committee, much less the House or the Senate, for impeachment. But we went ahead anyway, exploring the law and the facts in a responsible, honest manner.

An impeachment inquiry is not, and should not be, a "gotcha" proceeding. It's a process for searching for and finding and airing the facts to determine whether they satisfy the constitutional requirements for overturning the results of an election and removing a president from office. As in a trial, you must put your case together fact by fact, legal argument by legal argument, and put it to a jury to decide. You simply work hard and trust the process. That's how the House Judiciary Committee operated in 1974, and that is how impeachment should operate now. Obviously, you can't start the process without evidence of significant and egregious presidential wrongdoing, but starting it is not the same thing as deciding the president should be impeached. Once begun, you must be willing to say we can't impeach if the evidence or the law doesn't stand up after a proper and thorough inquiry. Similarly, if the evidence and law do stand up, you must then be willing to say that we should impeach.

I know that in these partisan times, saying something like that sounds naïve. It's clear that I do not like President Trump and that I think there is a great deal of evidence supporting his potential impeachment. But calling for an impeachment inquiry can work if we take what we did in the President Nixon impeachment as a model. I did not like Nixon very much, either, but "likes" and "dislikes" were put aside in favor of a process that was fair and honorable. I believe that we should embark on that process for President Trump—a man who I believe threatens our democracy.

The following chapters explore the constitutional law regarding impeachments, the three major charges against President Trump that I believe currently have the most evidentiary and legal support, and finally several other presidential misdeeds that may or may not warrant further inquiry. I want to add one important caveat: much of what I recount is from news reports and is not the product of a thoroughgoing congressional investigation by a committee using subpoena power. Moreover, new facts and details emerge constantly—facts that may help exonerate or inculpate the president—making it likely that within a matter of days, if not hours, portions of this book will have failed to include important developments—or become outdated. Nevertheless, I believe that the broad outlines of the story of President Trump's abuses are clear—and mandate that we begin the important work of making sure that no president is above the law.

2

"Great and Dangerous Offenses": The Standard for Impeachment

The framers of our Constitution knew that someday there would be a president who would threaten the foundations of our democracy. They didn't know if his name would be Richard Nixon or Donald Trump, or what guise his misdeeds would take, but they knew that the American people would need a remedy. Waiting years until the next election to remove from office a president who engages in grave misconduct would pose a danger to the country. Thus, the framers provided for the removal of a president through impeachment, a centuries-old process with deep roots in British history.

The grounds for impeachment specified in the Constitution are grave ones that strike at the heart of our system of government: "The President, Vice President and all civil Officers of the United States, shall be removed from Office on Impeachment for, and Conviction of, Treason, Bribery, or other high Crimes and Misdemeanors."

Treason is defined in the Constitution. It means "levying War against [the United States], or . . . adhering to their Enemies, giving them Aid and Comfort" (Article III, Section 3). *Bribery*, although undefined, seemed relatively clear. It was well understood by the framers—and is generally well understood now, though as we will see briefly in Chapter 5, today's federal criminal law governing bribery is very cramped.

But what are *high Crimes and Misdemeanors?* The phrase was added late in drafting the Constitution. When the framers first considered an impeachment clause at the Constitutional Convention in Philadelphia, they did not even debate before unanimously adopting a provision allowing impeachment for "malpractice or neglect of duty." Later, however, some convention delegates had second thoughts. Pennsylvania's Gouverneur Morris and South Carolina's George Pinckney pushed to strike the entire provision, arguing there was no need for impeachment, that elections would solve the problem. Virginia delegate George Mason scoffed. "Shall any man be above justice?" he asked. "Above all, shall that man be above it who can commit the most extensive injustice?" James Madison, who played a pivotal role in drafting the Constitution and served later as our fourth president, could think of many reasons for an impeachment provision. It was "indispensable," he said, arguing that a president might otherwise "pervert his administration into a scheme of peculation or oppression. He might betray his trust to foreign powers." Morris and Pinckney were beaten back. The impeachment clause would stay in the Constitution. A new version of the provision—closer to the one we know today—was offered, but solely for treason or bribery. Mason proposed adding "maladministration," but his suggestion was rebuffed as too vague. He then suggested adding "high crimes and misdemeanors" to the impeachment clause.

Why was he so persistent? He realized—and the framers ultimately concurred—that an impeachment provision that dealt only with "treason" and "bribery" was not broad enough to encompass the various kinds of serious harm a president could inflict on the country. Mason warned there would be "many great and dangerous offenses" and "attempts to subvert the Constitution" that would not be covered by treason or bribery. These needed to be covered.

To drive home his argument, Mason pointed to the notorious contemporary example of Warren Hastings, the British governor general of India who was impeached by Parliament just a few months before the start of the Constitutional Convention. As Harvard Law School professor Cass Sunstein explains in his useful book *Impeachment: A Citizen's Guide,* Hastings was accused of a wide variety of misdeeds, in particular personal corruption, maladministration, and "exercising arbitrary power, disregarding treaty obligations, selling favors, and engaging in fraud and corruption in making contracts."

Mason worried that the behavior Hastings had exhibited and with which the framers were immediately familiar would not be impeachable under the phrasing of the constitutional provision as then written. He also pointed out that the Constitution banned bills of attainder, which the Supreme Court has defined as "legislative punishment, of any form or severity, of specifically designated persons or groups." Congress, Mason noted, could not punish such wrongdoing by a particular president. Thus, "it is the more necessary to extend: the power of impeachments," he argued.

Mason wanted to expand the scope of impeachment to cover more kinds of executive misconduct, the kind that Hastings engaged in and that a bill of attainder would encompass. He ultimately proposed adding to treason and bribery the phrase "other high Crimes and Misdemeanors agst. the State." The proposal was adopted, though the words "agst. the State" were later dropped.

The framers were practical people. They understood the dangers a president could pose, even in a four-year period. They had lived under a British monarch and had no illusions.

Flash forward almost two hundred years to the President Nixon impeachment proceedings. After much analysis, most Judiciary Committee members decided in 1974 that high crimes and misdemeanors—like treason and bribery—meant "injuries done immediately to the society itself," as Alexander Hamilton explained in 1788 in *Federalist* paper No. 65. No criminal conduct, a bipartisan majority of the committee believed, was necessary to satisfy that standard.

This 1974 view is important in understanding what is impeachable, because it represents the only time in American history that the impeachment clause was deployed against a president in a principled and bipartisan way. The 1974 articles represent the one democratically valid example we have of a living, breathing interpretation of high crimes and misdemeanors and reflect the considered and heartfelt opinion of men and women who had real democratic responsibility and accountability as they lived through a constitutional crisis. The articles therefore should be accorded substantial weight.

In July 1974, the House Judiciary Committee approved three articles of impeachment on a bipartisan basis. (See Appendix II.) Article II listed the president's acts that merited impeachment: he was charged with authorizing illegal wiretaps of journalists and White House staffers and using the information for his own political goals; ordering IRS audits of opponents of his Vietnam War policies (the Enemies List) as retaliation; allowing the creation of a special White House investigative unit (the Plumbers) to break into Daniel Ellsberg's psychiatrist's office to smear the man who had leaked the Pentagon Papers; and impeding lawful investigations into Watergate for purposes that had nothing to do with the welfare of the country. President Nixon, the Judiciary Committee said, "has repeatedly engaged in conduct violating the constitutional rights of citizens, impairing the due and proper administration of justice and the conduct of lawful inquiries, or contravening the laws governing agencies of the executive branch and the purpose of these agencies."

Article I charged that President Nixon "prevented, obstructed, and impeded the administration of justice" with respect to the investigation and prosecution of those responsible for the Watergate break-in. President Nixon's acts of impeding and obstructing included authorizing hush-money payments and offering presidential pardons to the burglars to keep them from telling the prosecutors the whole story; ordering the firing of the Watergate special prosecutor to prevent him from obtaining White House tapes (later shown to be extremely damaging to President Nixon) and to stymie his investigation; directing perjury by a top aide before a Senate committee; obtaining grand jury information from the Department of Justice and using that information to help aides avoid prosecution; and trying to get the CIA to stop the FBI's investigation into the break-in, using a phony claim of national security. The very same acts that were impeachable as a cover-up were impeachable as an abuse of power in Article II.

Finally, Article III was adopted, with just two votes from Republicans. It involved, as we have seen, President Nixon's scorn for the role of Congress in the impeachment process, in particular his failure to comply with subpoenas issued by the House Judiciary Committee for documents and tapes. If presidents could block an impeachment inquiry's effort to get at the facts, they might be able to block impeachment altogether. All of this was "contrary to his trust as President and subversive of constitutional government, to the great prejudice of the cause of law and justice, and to the manifest injury of the people of the United States," as each of the articles concluded. In August 1974, after the tapes, including Nixon's Oval Office smoking-gun conversations, were finally released to the Judiciary Committee as a result of a Supreme Court ruling, all the Republicans who had previously voted against the articles announced that they were now prepared to vote for Nixon's impeachment.

The three articles lay out the facts and patterns of behavior that demonstrate the meaning of "high crimes and misdemeanors." In my opinion, the definition we can glean from those articles and the Nixon impeachment process itself is that high crimes and misdemeanors covers egregious and grave abuses of power that threaten the rule of law or the liberties of Americans.

This is not very different from the definition advanced by many scholars, as we shall see later.

Many looking at the phrase "high crimes and misdemeanors" jump to the conclusion that a president must have committed a crime in order to be impeached, a view most recently advocated by Professor Alan Dershowitz, in *The Case Against Impeaching Trump*. Dershowitz was my professor at Harvard Law School. He and I have maintained a friendly relationship over the years, though we often diverge politically. His thesis, however—and I say this with all the respect due a former Harvard instructor—is wrong.

Professor Dershowitz is a defense counsel par excellence, whose verbal gymnastics in support of President Trump are matched by those of Rudolph Giuliani, the president's widely televised lawyer, who regularly asserts that a president cannot commit crimes. According to Giuliani, a president cannot obstruct justice because a president cannot commit a crime as long as he is acting within his powers as president—assertions that echo President Nixon's infamous statement: "Well, when the president does it, that means that it is not illegal." Moreover, according to Giuliani, a president cannot be indicted while in office. In these two advocates, President Trump has found a get-out-of-impeachment-free card: he can be impeached only for crimes, but a president cannot commit crimes. Presto.

The framers would be appalled.

It is entirely predictable that President Trump's supporters would want to create significant obstacles to his removal from office. Professor Dershowitz seeks to transform impeachment into a criminal proceeding, importing the trappings of a criminal trial into the process, including a requirement that a president's guilt be proven beyond a reasonable doubt. He argues that the Constitution's "explicit words . . . require conviction of a specified crime as a prerequisite to impeachment." In fact, no words require that, nor has any impeachment proceeding against a president ever raised that as a condition.

The framers, as we have seen, struggled to strike a balance between making impeachment too easy, and thereby weakening the presidency, and making impeachment available to remove a dangerous president. After several attempts, they arrived at the solution we have today: three specified grounds for impeachment (treason, bribery, and other high crimes and misdemeanors), a vote of a majority of the House of Representatives to impeach, and a two-thirds vote of the Senate to convict. We don't need to make the impeachment process harder than they did. As it is, the process of impeachment is so difficult and cumbersome that no president has ever been removed through impeachment alone. President Nixon would have been the exception to the rule, but he short-circuited the process by resigning.

The weight of evidence against Professor Dershowitz's opinion is great. Still, it is important to expose the flaws in his thinking, because the claim he makes crops up repeatedly from those defending a president who faces possible impeachment.

His argument—that a president must commit a crime to be impeached—is not true. I know that from my own experience as a member of the House Judiciary Committee that voted to impeach President Nixon, a proceeding that rejected the position that a crime was needed for impeachment. It also runs counter to the history of impeachment in England and the American colonies, the debates surrounding the adoption of the provision at the Constitutional Convention, the opinions of those who ratified the Constitution, and other writings of that time. Furthermore, many major constitutional scholars believe no crime is required for impeachment.

Making it impossibly hard to impeach and remove a president also runs directly counter to the objectives of the framers, who wanted impeachment available and usable to protect America's democracy. They were worried that a president could become a tyrant and/or sell out the country to foreign interests.

Mason and Madison, as detailed above, were emphatic about the need to have a usable impeachment process. Others at the convention also explained the need for the power. Virginia's Edmund Randolph, who later became our nation's first attorney general, warned that "[t]he Executive will have great opportunities of abusing his power . . ." Impeachment, he believed, was a tool to save us from that abuse. There was no mention by any of these men of the need for crimes to impeach.

Former president Gerald Ford, when he was House minority leader and led the effort to impeach the great Supreme Court Justice William O. Douglas, famously proclaimed that an "impeachable offense is whatever a majority of the House of Representatives considers it to be at a given moment in history." As with Professor Dershowitz, I do not agree with President Ford or believe the House or Senate may remove a president on a whim.

The constitutional grounds for impeachment must both exist and be proven to a majority of the House of Representative and two-thirds of the Senate before impeachment and removal can occur. So I am happy to say that there is something on which I completely agree with Professor Dershowitz. "If the formal process of [presidential] removal is to have legitimacy," he says, "it must be done in strict compliance with the provisions of the Constitution."

Where Professor Dershowitz and I disagree is on the meaning of "other high crimes and misdemeanors." The term may seem clear on its face, but it is not. He incorrectly construes it to mean a crime, although his error is understandable: Treason and bribery are generally understood to be crimes, and "high crimes and misdemeanors" sounds, too, as if it refers to criminal behavior. If, however, Professor Dershowitz had studied the history of the term's entry into the Constitution, he likely would have discovered his mistake.

According to Cass Sunstein, the wording was adopted so that impeachment would be directed at "serious criminality or the abuse or misuse of the responsibilities of *high* office" (emphasis mine). "High" is not a quantitative but a qualitative adjective. It does not mean "very bad." It means the sort of misdeeds committed by holders of high offices, not by ordinary people.

It is also important to recall how and why impeachment was inserted into the Constitution. As noted above, as the framers approached the end of the debate about impeachment, treason and bribery were the only grounds specified. Mason's protest that treason "will not reach many great and dangerous offenses" and that "[a]ttempts to subvert the Constitution may not be Treason" prompted the adoption of "high crimes and misdemeanors." The phrase *attempts to subvert the Constitution* is what "high crimes and misdemeanors" was partially intended to cover, and it is obvious that these attempts will not necessarily be criminal in nature. Efforts to subvert could involve abuses of power that are not criminal. Indeed, it's not even clear that the term *great and dangerous offenses* refers exclusively to crimes, either.

Overall, the historical record of the debate at the Constitutional Convention in Philadelphia shows that the impeachment provision was not meant to require a crime. After drafting, the Constitution was sent to the states for ratification, and again, the historical record is clear: in the state debates, as Professor Sunstein points out, impeachment was understood as a way of addressing "an egregious violation of the public trust while in office." Hamilton, one of the most respected commentators on the proposed Constitution, explained that impeachment involves "offenses which proceed from the misconduct of public men, or, in other words, from the abuse or violation of some public trust" (*Federalist* paper No. 65). Again, no reference to the requirement of a crime.

"In short, the debates at the Constitutional Convention show at least that impeachable offenses were not limited to indictable offenses," writes UNC–Chapel Hill law professor Michael J. Gerhardt, author of *The Federal Impeachment Process*. He finds the same to be true of the various state debates on ratification.

Congressional precedent is another factor to be considered. At the beginning of the House Judiciary Committee's impeachment inquiry into President Nixon, committee members were given a staff memorandum on the meaning of "high crimes and misdemeanors." The memo's conclusion was that impeachment did not require the commission of a crime. That issue was vigorously debated, and most committee members, including a number of Republicans, were persuaded that the memo was correct. (Excerpts from the memorandum can be found in Appendix I.)

None of the three articles of impeachment the Judiciary Committee adopted during Watergate explicitly charged Nixon with a crime, tracked the criminal code, or rested on any premise that Nixon had committed a crime. The first article dealt with Nixon's cover-up of the Watergate break-in. While using the phrase *obstructed . . . justice* (Nixon "prevented, obstructed and impeded the administration of justice"), the article neither spelled out the elements of the crime of obstruction of justice nor stated that Nixon had committed obstruction of justice or, in fact, any other crime. There is simply no claim that Nixon violated any criminal statute, only that he violated his oath of office and "his constitutional duty to take care that the laws be faithfully executed." Neither violation is a crime, nor can either violation be committed by an ordinary person. These are "political crimes" against the government committed by persons of high office in that government. That is why the article charged President Nixon with "high crimes and misdemeanors." The second article of impeachment dealt with Nixon's abuse of power, such as ordering the IRS to audit his political enemies. That order was not a crime.

The impeachment of President Bill Clinton also supports the position that impeachment is not synonymous with criminal behavior or conviction of a crime. The two articles of impeachment approved by the House of Representatives were grounded in criminal law matters, to be sure: assertions that the president had lied under oath and had obstructed justice. But as the leaders of the House impeachment inquiry put it in their memorandum to the Senate, "The ultimate issue is whether the President's course of conduct is such as to affect adversely the Office of the President and also upon the administration of justice, and whether he has acted in a manner contrary to his trust as President and subversive to the Rule of Law and Constitutional government." I believe that the Clinton impeachment was an abuse of power by the House of Representatives and that his behavior did not rise to the level set by the House leaders or the Constitution. Also, President Clinton did not use the powers of his office to engage in the misconduct with which he was charged.

It should also be noted that the impeachment of President Andrew Johnson centered on his disregarding a statute that required him to obtain Senate approval before he could remove a Senate-confirmed cabinet officer from office. There was no violation of the criminal law involved in that impeachment, which, perhaps because of its highly partisan character, failed in the Senate.

Other highly regarded scholars of impeachment who have studied the issue in depth find no requirement of a crime. Yale Law School professor Charles L. Black Jr., in his iconic *Impeachment: A Handbook*, defines "high crimes and misdemeanors" as follows:

> I think we can say that high Crimes and Misdemeanors, in the constitutional sense, ought to be held to be those offenses which are rather obviously wrong, whether or not "criminal," and which so seriously threaten the order of political society as to make pestilent and dangerous the continuation in power of their perpetrator.

Harvard law professor Raoul Berger, in his authoritative work *Impeachment: The Constitutional Problems*, tracks the development in Britain of the term "high crimes and misdemeanors" from the fourteenth century and argues persuasively that it did not refer to ordinary crimes but rather to acts against the state or government.

Professor Sunstein, who recently addressed the issue, contends that impeachment does not require a criminal act. "Impeachment is available for egregious abuses of official authority. Some crimes do not count as such because they are essentially private (failing to pay taxes . . .) or because they are not sufficiently serious. Some offenses that are not crimes are nonetheless impeachable—punishing political enemies, trampling on liberty," he notes. Noted constitutional expert Professor Laurence Tribe refutes the idea as well that impeachment requires criminal behavior, and in *To End a Presidency*, he and Joshua Matz define high crimes and misdemeanors as follows: "like treason and bribery, they involve corruption, betrayal, or an abuse of power that subvert core tenets of the US governmental system."

The simple truth is a president can be impeached both for things that are crimes and things that are not. Not all crimes are impeachable.

———

After making his faulty claim that a president can be impeached only for a crime, Professor Dershowitz goes on to analyze the possible criminal claims against Trump. There, too, his argument is deficient. For example, he asserts that no "deal was made" by Trump or his campaign with the Russians in return for their providing dirt on Hillary Clinton. Perhaps that is so, but how does he know? Obviously, he can't he sure. I argue later in this book that there is sufficient evidence, both circumstantial and direct, to raise a substantial concern about whether a "deal was made." Either way, we cannot simply accept Professor Dershowitz's unproven claim that there was no deal and then move on. The question whether such a bargain was made is so significant that it must be fully investigated.

Professor Dershowitz raises another argument against impeachment: that a congressionally created commission such as the 9/11 Commission could investigate instead of a special counsel or prosecutor. He even goes so far as to say that special counsel Mueller should hold his investigation in abeyance while that happens. This is a convenient argument for a pro-Trump advocate. Since a president cannot be impeached until convicted of a crime, as Professor Dershowitz contends, shutting down a criminal investigation creates a very easy way to avoid impeachment altogether.

And what are the reasons Professor Dershowitz offers for this interruption of Mueller's investigation? The public is "losing faith" in Mueller, and a commission could be a better way of learning the "whole truth." If the public is, in fact, losing faith in Mueller, it is a direct result of the baseless attacks by President Trump on his investigation—attacks that appear designed to impede and undermine the investigation and may themselves be a crime or impeachable abuse of power. No president should be able to avoid a criminal investigation—and criminal charges—simply by relentlessly attacking the prosecutor.

Nor is it clear that a commission would be better able to get the whole truth. There is no reason to believe that President Trump would honor a commission's subpoenas for his documents and testimony, and it is also unclear whether the Supreme Court would enforce them. In the Nixon tapes case, it was a grand jury subpoena the Supreme Court upheld, favoring the needs of the criminal justice system over presidential claims for nondisclosure.

A commission promises a cathartic truth-seeking effort without the unpleasant need to hold people accountable, and impeachment, after all, is a harsh act. Without proper limits, without standards, and in the wrong hands in Congress, it is a dangerous tool. Not as dangerous, I would argue, as an unchecked, autocratic president. But, still, threatening.

That said, an impeachment does not deprive anyone of liberty or life, which conviction of a crime potentially does. At worst, it deprives someone of a job through a vote by senators and representatives, and the process has two substantial safeguards as well: Each of the senators and representatives will have to stand for election before the people and defend his or her vote. And in a presidential impeachment, the vice president, duly elected, becomes president, which means that the party in power remains in power.

But if a president were to subvert the constitution or commit great and dangerous offenses? Sometimes, it turns out, we just really need to be able to fire him or her.

3

Failure to Protect the Integrity of
Our Federal Election Process

Russia engaged in information warfare against the United States in 2016 in order to tamper with the presidential election. It does not matter why it did so or which candidate it supported (though it did in fact support Donald Trump). It does not matter whether its attacks actually affected the outcome, though many suspect they did. A hostile foreign nation attacked our nation's vital election infrastructure and manipulated public attitudes about the candidates and influenced hot-button issues and even people's decisions whether or not to vote. There are only two suitable responses: unequivocal condemnation and a vigorous defense. President Trump has done neither. His outright refusal to defend and protect us against these attacks is a potentially impeachable failure "to preserve, protect and defend the Constitution of the United States," which rests above all else on the fair and honest election of a president, vice-president, and members of Congress.

A president's words and actions when our country is under attack are of the gravest importance. But President Trump has not condemned or even unambiguously acknowledged Russia's sustained and sophisticated attack on the 2016 election, and he has failed to develop a comprehensive plan to counter ongoing and future attacks. He has been more than recalcitrant: he encouraged efforts to assault our democracy and has actively undermined viable efforts to protect our election system.

The Russian assault on our election in 2016 was a cyber Pearl Harbor. If the Russians had aimed missiles at us instead of electronic pulses at our voting booths and social media, the demands for swift and decisive presidential action would be overwhelming. But the president has muted this reaction by a web of deceptions about Russia's role and the damage it caused, leaving us vulnerable as a nation to further interference in the future.

The Russian government thus continues to engage in cyberwarfare against the United States, following much the same playbook as in 2016: Our election systems are being tested by Russian intrusions. Government officials and candidates are being targeted for hacking. New social media campaigns to foment crisis are under way. More recently, the Russians have begun cyber incursions into our nation's electrical and power grids.

In his responses (or lack thereof), President Trump has:

> First, disregarded his responsibilities as commander in chief to repel and prevent attacks on our country, including cyberattacks;

> Second, shunned his constitutional responsibility in Article II, Section 3, of the Constitution to "take Care that the Laws be faithfully executed";

> Third, impaired the basic constitutional right of Americans to fair and honest elections;

> Fourth, systematically made false and misleading public statements for the purpose of deceiving the American people about the identity of the attackers and his knowledge of the attacks; and

> Fifth, withheld relevant and material evidence, information, or assistance from the intelligence community, which was trying to block the Russian attacks in 2016.

Taken together, these violations of constitutional duty are grounds for impeachment.

ATTACKS ON THE 2016 ELECTION

Russia's cyberattacks on the American election infrastructure and public opinion were sophisticated and serious, involving more than zeros and ones. Millions of dollars were spent. Hostile actors entered American territory and stole identities of American citizens. They infiltrated America's political institutions. They broke numerous US laws.

The attacks focused on three fronts:

An effort to break into the nation's election machinery;

Theft and distribution of confidential information to hurt the Hillary Clinton campaign; and

Use of social media, combined with Russia-funded and Russia-initiated events and rallies, to sow political discord, heighten racial tension, and influence the election outcome by depressing voter turnout for Clinton and increasing it for Trump.

We know from three prominent sources that the Russian government assaulted the 2016 elections:

American intelligence agencies investigated the attacks and are unanimous that they came from Russia.

The Department of Justice (DOJ) has indicted twenty-six Russians (a subset of the thirty-four people in total whom Mueller indicted) and three companies for the attacks, laying out detailed evidence in support of its allegations.

Three major social media companies—Facebook, Google, and Twitter—conducted their own investigations and concluded that Russian manipulation occurred.

THE INTELLIGENCE COMMUNITY CONCLUSIONS

On January 6, 2017, the Office of the Director of National Intelligence released a declassified report on the Russian assault. Reflecting the combined judgment of the DNI and the heads of the National Security Agency, the FBI, and the CIA, it found:

> Russian efforts to influence the 2016 US presidential election represent the most recent expression of Moscow's longstanding desire to undermine the US-led liberal democratic order, but these activities demonstrated a significant escalation in directness, level of activity, and scope of effort compared to previous operations.
>
> . . . Russian President Vladimir Putin ordered an influence campaign in 2016 aimed at the US presidential election. . . .
>
> . . . Moscow will apply lessons learned from its Putin-ordered campaign aimed at the US presidential election to future influence efforts worldwide, including against US allies and their election processes.

Since then, the heads of the major intelligence agencies—every single one appointed by President Trump—have concurred in the judgment and warned of ongoing efforts to strike at our democracy.

- In June 2017, the Trump-appointed then-director of the CIA, Mike Pompeo, said: "I am confident that the Russians meddled in this election, as is the entire intelligence community."
- In May 2018, Trump-appointed secretary of homeland security Kirstjen Nielsen said: "We see [Russia] continuing to conduct foreign influence campaigns."
- In July 2018, Trump-appointed FBI director Christopher Wray said: "The intelligence community's assessment has not changed. My view has not changed, which is that Russia attempted to interfere with the last election and that it continues to engage in malign influence operations to this day."
- In August 2018, Trump-appointed director of national intelligence Dan Coats said: "We continue to see a pervasive messaging campaign by Russia to try to weaken and divide the United States."

- From 2017 through 2018, the Senate Select Committee on Intelligence conducted an independent review of the intelligence community's conclusions. Committee members held extensive hearings with the intelligence community heads and reviewed the documents that provided the foundation for the conclusion that Russia had assailed our election system in 2016. The committee is headed by a Republican senator from North Carolina, Richard Burr, and it determined that the findings contained in the January 2017 report were sound and that no political pressure was placed on any of the report's authors.

- Finally, a March 2018 report issued by the House Permanent Select Committee on Intelligence also concluded that Russia engaged in a "multifaceted" attack on the United States and that Russia believes it is "engaged in an information war with the West."

THE DEPARTMENT OF JUSTICE INDICTMENTS

Federal grand juries convened by the DOJ have criminally charged twenty-six people and three companies relating to their actions in 2016 in three separate indictments. The indictments provide detailed evidence of how Russia manipulated social media during the 2016 election, broke into the computer systems of Democratic Party organizations, and used Maria Butina, a spy posing as a student, to infiltrate the American political system on behalf of Russian officials. The goals of these efforts—to destabilize American democracy—could not be clearer.

On February 16, 2018, the first of the three indictments was filed by the office of special counsel Robert Mueller. It dealt with the social media attacks by Russia orchestrated in large part by a Russian troll farm called the Internet Research Agency, which is linked at the "highest levels" to the Kremlin. The indictment detailed the actions of companies and individual Russians. The Russians posed as Americans, created false American identities, and built social media accounts and groups to attract real Americans. The Facebook pages and Twitter accounts they fashioned were sharply honed to press divisive social and political causes.

As time wore on, these accounts, controlled by the Russian government, attracted "significant numbers of Americans for purposes of interfering with the US political system, including the presidential election of 2016," according to the indictment.

On July 13, 2018, a second indictment was issued by the office of the special counsel. This time, it dealt with efforts by officers of the Russian military intelligence unit called the Main Intelligence Directorate (GRU) of the General Staff. They are the individuals who hacked into the computer systems of three major Democratic Party organizations and several state boards of elections. We know their names, their ranks, their exact roles. We even know what they said to one another in emails. The specific detail presented in the indictment is overwhelming. The Russian military attacked our nation.

Finally, on July 17, 2018, the Department of Justice indicted Maria Butina. The indictment alleges that she worked at the direction of a high-level official in the Russian government to try to influence an organization thought to be the National Rifle Association in order to advance Russian interests.

SOCIAL MEDIA COMPANY INVESTIGATIONS

As concern about Russian efforts mounted in 2017, Facebook, Google, and Twitter conducted independent inquiries, later reporting their results. Executives of the three companies testified before Congress and confirmed that their investigations had found that Russian actors had used their services to interfere with the US election.

On October 2, 2017, Google general counsel Kent Walker announced that its investigation "found some evidence of efforts to misuse our platforms during the 2016 US election by actors linked to the Internet Research Agency in Russia."

On October 30, 2017, Joel Kaplan, Facebook's vice president for US public policy, told reporters: "The ads and accounts we found appeared to amplify divisive political issues across the political spectrum," including gun rights, gay rights issues, and the Black Lives Matter movement.

On January 19, 2018, Twitter confirmed that it had "identified and suspended a number of accounts potentially connected to a propaganda effort by a Russian government-linked organization known as the Internet Research Agency."

The joint intelligence community report of January 2017, the three indictments, and the social media company investigations offer just a glimpse of the scope of Russia's activity. There is much more that the public is not privy to. The intelligence report was issued only as a declassified paper, with substantial details omitted for security reasons. The Justice Department indictments focus narrowly on cases where prosecutors believe they have sufficient evidence to convict beyond a reasonable doubt. The social media companies have stated that they have not identified the full extent of the Russian measures. A clear narrative has nonetheless emerged from these sources and from press reports.

How Russia Attacked the United States

Front One: Our Voting Systems

America's election system is complex and diverse. There is no single administration, and our systems lack uniformity. Every state runs elections according to its own unique standards, different deadlines apply, and multiple types of equipment are used. All told, there as many as 7,500 voting administration authorities across the nation.

Our system is paradoxically both resilient and vulnerable to attack. Its resilience results from the multiple election authorities at work: a hack on a Texas system would not likely work in Connecticut. It may well not even work throughout Texas, since the systems used across the state's many counties and cities are varied. Yet the systems are also vulnerable because they are underfunded and localized, often lacking security expertise.

Russia carefully studied and exploited these vulnerabilities. From 2014 through the 2016 elections, its agents targeted at least eighteen states, and possibly another three, testing for weaknesses and attempting to gain access to voter registration systems. In six cases, they did gain entry. They targeted almost every part of the nation's election structures: voter registration systems, state and local election databases, the electronic roll books used at voting precincts to verify a voter's status, and voting equipment. In one state, thought to be Illinois, the Russian hackers illegally accessed the information of 500,000 voters, including their names, addresses, dates of birth, driver's license numbers, and partial social security numbers. Bloomberg has reported that investigators in Illinois saw evidence that the hackers tried to delete or alter voter data.

In Arizona, Russian hackers attempted to breach the state's voter registration database. The attack forced the state to take large portions of its entire election administration system offline for ten days in the summer of 2016, thankfully well before an actual election. Nevertheless, the fundraising efforts and campaigns of more than fifty candidates for political office were affected.

In addition, Russian military intelligence launched a cyberattack on voting equipment manufacturer VR Systems in the summer of 2016. The GRU accessed their computers and sent fraudulent emails from a fake company account to 122 election jurisdictions attempting to lure the recipients into installing malware.

According to the Senate Intelligence Committee, foreign enemy hackers were "in a position to, at a minimum, alter or delete voter registration data" for some of those hacked systems.

Front Two: Our Political Candidates and Organizations

As with our election systems, our candidate and political party operations are diverse. Often ad hoc and built to last only the brief time until the election, their level of cyber sophistication varies significantly.

In the year leading up to the 2016 election, the Russian government turned its sights on both Republican and Democratic Party organizations with the goal of stealing information from candidates and parties and divulging it to cause maximum damage. Using almost every tool in the hackers' toolkit, it methodically homed in on multiple targets at every governmental level, from mayors and governors to presidential candidates. Though it succeeded with both Republican and Democratic organizations, it used only what was stolen from Democratic ones. The top Democratic Party organizations, Clinton's top advisers, and more than 130 other party employees, contractors, and supporters were particularly in the crosshairs.

The most widely known attacks were on the servers and computers of the Democratic National Committee (DNC), which oversees the presidential nominating process. In mid-June 2016, the DNC publicly disclosed it had been hacked and told the public the attack was Russia-based. It began working to repair the damage, scrapping more than 140 servers and rebuilding the operating systems of more than 180 computers infected with malware that allowed the Russians to log every keystroke made by DNC personnel and to take screenshots. Several gigabytes of data were stolen; emails, documents, chats, and recordings were accessed; and personal banking records of some people were obtained.

Shortly after the DNC went public, Russian agents, posing as a solo hacker named Guccifer 2.0, claimed responsibility and leaked an opposition research report on Trump to the press. Guccifer 2.0 continued leaking documents and transferred a large data cache weeks later to WikiLeaks, an organization that Mike Pompeo—President Trump's CIA director—called a "hostile intelligence service."

WikiLeaks published almost 20,000 DNC emails on July 22, 2016, just days before the Democratic convention began in Philadelphia, timed to cause maximum tension between Bernie Sanders and Hillary Clinton supporters. They hit the mark, provoking a Florida lawsuit against the DNC and ultimately the resignation of the head of the DNC slightly more than three months before the election—both a major disruption for the party.

Russian military intelligence officers also hacked the Democratic Congressional Campaign Committee (DCCC), the top fund-raising organization for candidates for the House of Representatives, again obtaining emails and documents. The hackers even rewrote the DCCC website's underlying code to misdirect donors to a phony campaign contribution payment site. As with the DNC, the Russian government hackers released the material via Guccifer 2.0.

In the spring of 2016, Russia obtained access to the emails of Clinton campaign chair John Podesta using one of the easiest yet most effective hacking tools: a false email that looked like it came from Google asking Podesta to change his password. At least 50,000 of his emails were transmitted to WikiLeaks, which began releasing them on October 7, 2016. That was the day the notorious *Access Hollywood* video (recording candidate Trump's boast that he grabbed women by their genitals) was released. The Podesta emails were made public in a steady drip over the next weeks, distracting from an otherwise devastating Trump story. At the time, Guccifer 2.0 wrote to one reporter: "Together with Assange we'll make america [sic] great again."

Front Three: The Assault on Social Media

More than 75 percent of Americans have a social media account. For many, it is a means not only to communicate with friends, but to get news. What better way to inject turmoil into our democracy than through social media? The Russians used multiple social media tools (ads, groups, and viral organic posts) and platforms (Facebook, Twitter, Instagram, and Google) to undermine American civic and electoral participation. To generate conflict and depress turnout, they used hot-button issues like immigration, police misconduct, race, and religion. We still do not know the full extent of their efforts or their impact.

The Russians characterized their social media actions as "information warfare against the United States of America." The indictment brought by Mueller against Russian firms and individuals offers a window into this activity, chronicling a systematic effort begun in 2014. By mid-2016, the Russians had about eighty people working on the project in St. Petersburg and a budget of more than $1 million a month devoted to this endeavor. The indictment shows deliberate and methodical preparations, including visiting the United States for information-gathering purposes.

In October 2017 testimony before Congress, social media company executives laid out what Russia had done. One hundred twenty-six million American Facebook users were exposed to more than 80,000 inflammatory posts and more than $100,000 in advertisements. Russia uploaded more than 1,000 videos with more than 300,000 views on the American election to Google's YouTube service. Twitter published 1.4 million tweets from more than 30,000 Russian-backed accounts. All three companies have noted that the activity continues; in January 2018, Twitter set the number of automated accounts linked to the Russian government at 50,000. More than 677,775 people "followed one of these accounts or retweeted or liked a tweet from these accounts" from the beginning of September to mid-November 2016.

Essentially, social media was used to disseminate anti-Clinton and pro-Trump messages that appeared to be from Americans. They were designed to build on and foment anti-black and anti-Muslim sentiment—and to suppress the black vote for Hillary Clinton or encourage a vote for Green Party candidate Jill Stein. They also helped organize pro-Trump rallies in Florida, New York, and Pennsylvania.

A study by a University of Wisconsin professor analyzed how the Internet Research Agency tried to suppress nonwhite voter turnout by utilizing Facebook advertising. Identifying nonwhite voters a week before the election using benign ads focused on Martin Luther King Jr. and Beyoncé, it sent voter suppression ads to their Facebook pages on Election Day. "No one represents Black people," one such ad read. "Don't go to vote."

In the State of Washington, Russians on Facebook created an organization called United Muslims of America in July 2016 and planned a rally called "Support Hillary. Save American Muslims." They had someone hold a sign falsely attributing the quotation "I think Sharia Law will be a powerful new direction of freedom" to Hillary Clinton. Photos of the sign were posted on Twitter and Instagram. In Florida, Russians paid an American man $1,000 to build a cage for "jailing" a woman dressed as Clinton at a rally. They later tried to hire him to take his cage to New York. He declined, but the woman, posing as an imprisoned Clinton, accepted the offer.

Much of Russia's efforts in the social media sphere seem juvenile, simplistic, or petty, but they clearly struck a chord. They preyed upon the worst fears and impulses in American politics and successfully degraded a great deal of American political discourse to abuse and acrimony. Given the narrow margin of Trump's victory and the psychological sophistication and reach of the Russian efforts, it is impossible to say that they had no impact on the outcome of the 2016 presidential election. The election was decided by 107,000 votes in Pennsylvania, Michigan, and Wisconsin, and as former director of national intelligence James Clapper notes: "It stretches credulity to conclude that Russian activity didn't swing voter decisions."

President Trump Has Been Fully Informed Russia Is Behind These Efforts

On January 6, 2017, the same day the intelligence agencies released their report on the Russian attack, the heads of the agencies met with President-elect Trump to brief him about it. President Trump was shown texts and emails from Russian military officers about their efforts to attack the election. He was given information from "a top-secret source close to Mr. Putin, who had described to the C.I.A. how the Kremlin decided to execute its campaign of hacking and disinformation."

According to press reports, his briefers believed that the President-elect was "grudgingly convinced," which makes his subsequent behavior the more troubling. Since that briefing, as noted above, every single cabinet-level intelligence official appointed by President Trump has concurred with the report's conclusions.

CANDIDATE AND PRESIDENT TRUMP'S ACTIONS

Encouraging Russian Attacks on the 2016 Election and
Hindering Efforts to Counter Them

President Trump's disturbing and potentially impeachable indifference to the integrity of our election system stretches back before the January 6 intelligence meeting on Russian activity. In July, a few weeks after he became the Republican presidential nominee, he was briefed by the FBI that Russia would try to spy on and infiltrate his campaign and urged to report any relevant information to federal law enforcement.

There had already been multiple contacts between his campaign and Russian officials, and more were to come. Prior to the election, the Trump campaign had at least eighty-seven documented contacts with Russia-linked operatives, including at least twenty-six meetings, according to the Moscow Project, a branch of the Center for American Progress. At least twenty-three high-level campaign officials and Trump advisers were aware of exchanges between the Trump team and Russia. None was reported to federal law enforcement or the intelligence community. The only person who reported any of these interactions to the US intelligence community in 2016 was not an American, not in the United States, and not a part of the Trump operation. It was Alexander Downer, the Australian ambassador to the United Kingdom, who learned of the interactions over drinks at a London bar from George Papadopoulos, then serving as one of five foreign policy advisers to the Trump campaign.

The best-known effort by Russia to infiltrate the Trump campaign occurred on June 9, 2016, when Trump's son Donald Trump Jr., his son-in-law, Jared Kushner, and campaign manager Paul Manafort met with five Russians or Russia-connected people who asserted they could provide documents and material harmful to Hillary Clinton. The participants have repeatedly claimed that the meeting produced no results, yet within three days, WikiLeaks head Julian Assange announced that his organization would be publishing leaked Clinton emails. Five days later, Russian intelligence agents, posing as Guccifer 2.0, released the first stolen document from the DNC. Within two days, reporters had begun linking the Guccifer 2.0 leaks to Russian intelligence. Six weeks after the meeting, WikiLeaks began publishing its gusher of the hacked DNC material. From September through October 2016, Donald Trump Jr. exchanged messages with WikiLeaks, at one point asking about rumors of future leaks damaging to Clinton or the Democrats.

Through most of 2016, US intelligence and law enforcement agencies were alarmed by Russian activity in relation to the election, according to the January 2017 report. The agencies were engaged in counterintelligence investigations and sought to deploy other countermeasures. Our nation was trying to stop Russian interference. Yet the Trump campaign hid vital information from these agencies, depriving them of the tools that could have helped them protect the nation's election apparatus from cyberattack.

We do not know whether these contacts between Trump's team and the Russians amount to outright conspiracy. Still, there is certainly a significant amount of circumstantial evidence that Trump's campaign coordinated with the agents of a foreign power for political gain in 2016. (Some of that activity is recounted in Chapters 4 and 6 of this book.) What is known is that even as concerns about Russian hacking were growing, Trump publicly touted the leaks, the leakers, and Russia in 2016. Five days after WikiLeaks made the stolen DNC email trove public, he said at a July 27 Florida press conference, "Russia, if you're listening, I hope you're able to find the 30,000 emails that are missing," referring to emails on Hillary Clinton's personal server that she categorized as personal and deleted.

It's important to parse Trump's statement to the press: aside from encouraging a foreign government to hack or at least publish the emails of a former secretary of state, he is acknowledging Russia as a key player in the hacks and WikiLeaks publication. Trump did not call on China, other individuals, or a 400-pound person in New Jersey to look for the emails. Trump extended this extraordinary invitation to Russia the day after the *New York Times* first reported that US intelligence agencies were confident the Russian government had hacked the emails and funneled them to WikiLeaks. Russia responded the next day, targeting the Clinton campaign (by homing in on the emails of seventy-six staffers) and, for the first time, Clinton's personal office.

The intelligence community issued its first public warning about Russian efforts on October 7, 2016. The Department of Homeland Security (DHS) and the Office of the Director of National Intelligence issued a joint statement announcing that the US intelligence community "is confident" that the Russian government hacked into emails of "US persons and institutions" and disclosed them "to interfere with the US election process."

Candidate Trump's reaction was to amp up praise of the leakers. "I love WikiLeaks," he said on October 10, 2016, and followed the next day with:

"This WikiLeaks stuff is unbelievable. You've got to read it!" In this final month of the campaign, in which WikiLeaks released the Podesta emails, Trump lavished attention and praise 160 times on the organization. Bear in mind WikiLeaks' connection with Russian interests. In the spring of 2012, the Russian government–funded TV network *RT* gave Julian Assange a television show. It was likely an important source of revenue at the time, since WikiLeaks had been cut off from access to MasterCard and Visa services. After Assange fled to the Ecuadorian embassy in London to avoid extradition to Sweden for questioning on sexual assault, *RT* announced a partnership with WikiLeaks.

Trump also made consistent efforts in 2016 to obscure Russia's role in the election and may well have further encouraged Russia and confused the American voter as to the seriousness of the issue. In June 2016, he asserted that the DNC had hacked itself. "We believe it was the DNC that did the 'hacking' as a way to distract from the many issues facing their deeply flawed candidate and failed party leader. Too bad the DNC doesn't hack Hillary Clinton's 33,000 missing emails." During a presidential debate in September 2016, he acknowledged Russia might have been behind the hacking but undercut the acknowledgement by saying: "But it could also be China. It could also be lots of other people. It also could be somebody sitting on their bed that weighs 400 pounds, okay?"

———

President Trump has consciously and continuously misled the American public about a matter of critical national security. As president, he is privileged to have seen the detailed, classified evidence of the Russian attack, which the voting public has not. But rather than using his power and position to guard our democracy or to inform American citizens truthfully, he has lied to them.

Here are sixteen examples that demonstrate a consistent and clear pattern of deception:

December 2016. In an interview with *TIME* magazine, President-elect Trump said: "I don't believe they interfered. . . . It could be Russia. And it could be China. And it could be some guy in his home in New Jersey. I believe that it could have been Russia and it could have been any one of many other people."

December 31, 2016. After President Obama imposed sanctions on the Russians for their interference in the election, President-elect Trump said: "And I know a lot about hacking. And hacking is a very hard thing to prove. So, it could be someone else."

January 6, 2017. President-elect Trump said: "Russia, China, other countries, outside groups and people are consistently trying to break through the cyber infrastructure of our governmental institutions."

April 2017. In an interview with CBS's John Dickerson, President Trump again touted his cybersecurity expertise and cast doubt on how agencies prove responsibility for cybercrimes. "Knowing something about hacking, if you don't catch a hacker, okay, in the act, it's very hard to say who did the hacking," Trump said. "With that being said, I'll go along with Russia. It could have been China. It could have been a lot of different groups." He called collusion allegations "a phony story," prompting Dickerson to ask, "You don't think it's phony that they, the Russians, tried to meddle in the election?" President Trump responded, "That I don't know. I don't know."

May 11, 2017. To NBC's Lester Holt, President Trump explained his decision to fire FBI director Comey: "When I decided to just do it, I said to myself, I said, 'You know, this Russia thing with Trump and Russia is a made-up story, it's an excuse by the Democrats for having lost an election that they should've won.'" Holt pressed him: "We . . . there's already—there's already intelligence from virtually every intelligence agency that yes, that happened." Trump conceded that election interference was serious but spoke of Russia's involvement conditionally, always using the word "if." He said: "I'll tell you this. If Russia or anybody else is trying to interfere with our elections, I think it's a horrible thing and I want to get to the bottom of it. And I want to make sure it will never, ever happen."

July 2017. After a lengthy private conversation with Putin at a Group of 20 meeting, President Trump conveyed without comment Putin's responses to the charge of election interference. "First questions—first 20, 25 minutes—I said, 'Did you do it?' He said, 'No, I did not, absolutely not.' I then asked him a second time, in a totally different way. He said, 'Absolutely not.' Somebody did say if he did do it, you wouldn't have found out about it. Which is a very interesting point," President Trump said.

September 22, 2017. Shortly after Facebook revealed that Russians had bought ads on its platform in 2016 and that it was working with investigators in the office of special counsel Mueller, President Trump dismissed the social media giant's findings. He tweeted: "The Russia hoax continues, now it's ads on Facebook. What about the totally biased and dishonest Media coverage in favor of Crooked Hillary?"

November 2017. During a trip to Asia in which he met with Putin, President Trump declared: "Every time he sees me he says, 'I didn't do that,' and I really believe that when he tells me that, he means it. . . . I think he is very insulted by it, which is not a good thing for our country." President Trump passed on Putin's lie without comment, and then lied himself by claiming Putin was "sincere" when he knew Putin was not.

November 2017. During the same Asia trip, President Trump denigrated the heads of the intelligence agencies who had prepared the January 2017 report. "[I]f you look at all of this stuff and you say, what's going on here? And then you hear it's 17 [intelligence] agencies. Well, it's three. And one is [former CIA director] Brennan and one is whatever. I mean, give me a break. They're political hacks."

February 18, 2018. In the wake of Mueller's indictment for the social media campaign, President Trump once again failed to condemn Russian actions and continued to sow confusion and doubt: "I never said that Russia did not meddle in the election. I said 'it may be Russia, or China or another country or group or it may be a 400-pound genius sitting in bed and playing with his computer.'"

March 6, 2018. At a press appearance with the Swedish prime minister, Trump declared: "The Russians had no impact on our votes whatsoever." But no such determination has been made by any government agency or any other body researching the issue, and President Trump knew that from his January 2017 briefing. He went on to say: "[C]ertainly, there was meddling [by the Russians] and probably there was meddling from other countries and maybe other individuals." This statement simply repeats comments made long ago that muddy the waters on Russia's responsibility for the interference.

June 28, 2018. President Trump once again passed on Russia's false messaging to the American public in a tweet. "Russia continues to say they had nothing to do with Meddling in our Election!" He then pivoted to promoting the idea that Hillary Clinton actually colluded with Russia and that the DNC hack was an inside job. "Where is the DNC Server, and why didn't Shady James Comey and the now disgraced FBI agents take and closely examine it? Why isn't Hillary/Russia being looked at? So many questions, so much corruption!"

July 16, 2018. After meeting with Putin in Helsinki, Finland, President Trump spoke at a joint press conference. He was asked whether he would denounce what happened in 2016 and warn Russia never to do it again. In response, he once again repudiated the American intelligence community as part of an effort to hide or minimize Russian interference. "My people came to me, Dan Coats came to me and some others and said they think it's Russia. I have President Putin. He just said it's not Russia. I will say this. I don't see any reason why it would be." To stop the uproar about his comments, the next day President Trump said he misspoke and claimed he meant to say "why it wouldn't be." Whether he meant to say "would" or "wouldn't" is irrelevant. Both formulations are evasive, and not a clear statement that Russia engaged in cyberattacks, as it had.

July 17, 2018. Faced with continuing furor, President Trump tried to explain away his Helsinki performance: "I accept our intelligence community's conclusion that Russia's meddling in the 2016 election took place," he conceded, then undercut with his pro forma: "It could be other people also. There's a lot of people out there."

July 22, 2018. President Trump tweeted: "So President Obama knew about Russia before the Election. Why didn't he do something about it? Why didn't he tell our campaign? Because it is all a big hoax, that's why, and he thought Crooked Hillary was going to win!!!"

August 21, 2018. President Trump returned to only conditional acknowledgment of Russia's attacks. Speaking of special counsel Mueller's investigation, he told Reuters that it "played right into the Russians—if it was Russia—they played right into the Russians' hands."

President Trump has clearly and persistently said that he rejects or does not care what the intelligence and law enforcement agencies have concluded about Russian interference in the election. He has sent a signal to the public, the agencies, and the world that he does not take the matter seriously as part of his effort to downplay and cover up Russia's interference. Russia surely has received the same signal and likely has concluded it is free to interfere again.

President Trump has tried to undermine public confidence in our election system in yet another way, by repeatedly spreading falsehoods about illegal voting and claiming that 3 million fraudulent ballots were cast in 2016. To support this deception, he created a Presidential Advisory Commission on Election Integrity to investigate the nation's voting systems. Focusing almost exclusively on fraud rather than security, the commission was disbanded less than nine months later, having never conducted comprehensive research, completed an investigation, produced a report, or offered any recommendations. The claim of fraud was not just laughable, but diverted attention from the real problem of Russian election interference.

———

President Trump's Failure to Provide Safeguards against Future Attacks

It took more than a year and a half after Inauguration Day for President Trump to chair a meeting of the National Security Council to discuss election security. The meeting was prompted by his disastrous performance at Helsinki, which he tried to minimize by creating the appearance that, despite everything, he actually cared about protecting our elections from Russian attack. When it finally came about, in late July 2018, the meeting lasted a scant thirty minutes. He "issued no new directives to counter or deter the threat," according to the *Washington Post*.

A commander in chief seeking to respond to a cyberattack has many options available, including imposing sanctions or other penalties, hardening or improving our defenses, and counterattacking. President Trump failed to direct the use of any of them at that July meeting—or at any other time before that.

In fact, President Trump has shied away from confronting the Russians or protecting the integrity of our elections from them. Almost immediately after winning the 2106 election, he and his team began undercutting efforts to respond to the Russian attack. On December 29, 2016, President Barack Obama announced measures to punish Russia for its interference in the presidential election, including the expulsion of Russian operatives from the United States and the imposition of new sanctions. President-elect Trump's transition office issued a statement: "It's time for our country to move on to bigger and better things." His team worked to undermine the sanctions, reassuring Sergey Kislyak, the Russian ambassador, that Russia would get a friendly hearing from the new administration. Jared Kushner was so eager for that friendly hearing that he asked Ambassador Kislyak to help set up back-channel communications using Russian diplomatic facilities "in an apparent move to shield their pre-inauguration discussions from monitoring" by the United States, according to the *Washington Post*. In the next chapter, we'll examine the actions of President Trump's first national security adviser, Michael Flynn, in regard to those sanctions.

President Trump's utterly inadequate response to Russia's election interference did not change after his inauguration. The most notable cybersecurity initiative he pursued occurred in July 2017. After meeting with Putin, President Trump hyped a joint US-Russia "impenetrable Cyber Security Unit" for elections. This fox-guarding-the-henhouse idea didn't pass the congressional smell test. It was "pretty close" to "the dumbest idea I've ever heard," according to Republican senator Lindsey Graham. It provoked fierce rebukes from other Republican senators, including a tweet from Marco Rubio: "Partnering with Putin on a 'Cyber Security Unit' is akin to partnering with Assad on a 'Chemical Weapons Unit.'" After the pushback, President Trump withdrew the idea. The proposal was another kind of deception: a way of suggesting that Russia was not a cyber adversary and could be trusted.

Congress's attempt to address the issue, an August 2017 law sanctioning Russia for its election interference, was resisted by President Trump. He wanted to veto the bill but was persuaded his veto would be overridden. For a long period of time thereafter, however, he simply did not implement the sanctions as directed by Congress.

President Trump not only failed to use sanctions in 2017, he neglected his responsibility to lead the government in appropriate countermeasures or in improving our defenses. By late 2017, the impact was becoming clear. In October 2017 congressional testimony, Attorney General Jeff Sessions was asked whether the administration had done enough to prevent future Russian assaults. "Probably not," he said. "And the matter is so complex that for most of us we are not able to fully grasp the technical dangers that are out there."

Our military and intelligence agencies were not mobilized to address the attacks. In February 13, 2018, testimony before the Senate Intelligence Committee, National Security Agency director Mike Rogers testified, "I can't say I've been directed to blunt or actually stop" Russian cyberassaults. The NSA is the main spy and defense agency charged with conducting cyber operations. In fact, all the heads of US intelligence agencies testified at the hearing that President Trump had not directed them specifically to combat Russian attacks on our election systems. FBI Director Wray, then-CIA director Pompeo, and Director of National Intelligence Coats "were unable to point to specific direction from President Trump to 'blunt' and 'disrupt' Russian meddling in future elections," according to a report from *The Hill*. In later February testimony before the Senate Armed Services Committee, Rogers testified that in the absence of a clear direction, he did not have the authority to respond to Russian interference. "I need a policy decision that indicates there is specific direction to do that. . . . I've never been given any specific direction to take additional steps outside my authority. I have taken the steps within my authority, you know, trying to be a good, proactive commander," Rogers said. "I have not been granted any additional authorities." He went on: "Clearly what we've done hasn't been enough."

At least one other agency that President Trump should have tasked with urgent action simply neglected its duty. On March 4, 2018, the *New York Times* reported that the State Department had not yet spent a penny of the $120 million it was allocated by Congress to counter election assaults by foreign agents. Not a single Russian-speaking analyst worked at that time in the bureau responsible for dealing with the problem. Likewise, the Department of Homeland Security has been dilatory in providing protection. At a March 2018 hearing regarding the department's work, Republican senator Susan Collins of Maine told Secretary Kirstjen Nielsen: "When I listen to your testimony, I hear no sense of urgency to really get on top of this issue." Indeed, the department did not notify states about its findings on 2016 interference until September 2017. "It's unacceptable that it took almost a year after the election to notify states that their elections systems were targeted," Democratic senator Mark Warner of Virginia added. In late July 2018, President Trump's former homeland security adviser, Tom Bossert, told Yahoo News he was worried about "who's minding the store" with respect to developing strategy for cybersecurity. "On cyber, there is no clear person and/ or clear driver, and there is no clear muscle memory," he said.

In the wake of President Trump's calamitous performance at his July 2018 Helsinki meeting with Putin, the administration scrambled to find examples of actions it was undertaking to combat Russian election interference. First, it staged a press conference with the heads of the US intelligence community, but President Trump notably did not attend. Then, it pointed out in a press release that the Department of Homeland Security was coordinating with state election officials and offering them free cybersecurity scans, but that was a puny move in the face of a concerted cyberattack by a hostile nation. The White House also cited in that press release its most substantive program to counter Russia's activities, but it turned out to be a congressionally mandated $380 million fund allocated four months earlier to help states upgrade their election systems. Most analysts believe it will cost three times that, and the allocation is not even specifically earmarked for security. As of August 2018, most state election officials said the money came too late to have a real impact on the elections.

A smattering of announcements followed the press release. In late July, the NSA announced a Russia Small Group to deal with cyberattacks but hastened to add that it was in line with previous activities and not a marked change in strategy. In August 2018, the FBI announced its Foreign Influence Task Force. Political campaigns have reported no systematic contact from it or from any law enforcement officials. There is no "sign that law enforcement is playing a proactive role to protect campaigns from meddling on a day-to-day basis," according to the *New York Times*.

Finally, in late September 2018, President Trump announced a new process for imposing sanctions in the event of future election interference. Many non-Democratic groups criticized the process as a Band-Aid. "Trump is way late to the game. The only reason this is happening is the tremendous amount of publicity and pressure he's now feeling about elections," Patrick Eddington, a national security analyst at the Cato Institute, a libertarian organization, told *Wired* magazine. "This isn't a serious policy initiative. If they were serious about trying to harden election defenses, this would have come the first week Trump got sworn into office and they would have coordinated with folks on the Hill and the congressional committee chairs."

Congressional responses to the ongoing threats have met with continuous opposition from President Trump. For example, until March 2018 he ignored a congressional mandate to impose sanctions on Russia, acting only after pressure from European allies and in response to the poisoning of a British resident. In imposing the sanctions, Trump himself never mentioned Russian election interference. Interference with our elections wasn't serious enough to impose a penalty on Russia.

President Trump has resisted Congress about more than sanctions. In early August 2018, the Secure Elections Act, crafted by Republican senator James Lankford of Oklahoma, was poised for passage a few weeks later. It would have granted state election officials security clearances for easier access to critical intelligence and required that states conduct election result audits, a vital tool for ensuring accurate outcomes and detecting interference. The White House opposed the bill, and it died. In hearings of the Senate Banking and Foreign Relations Committees that month, senators repeatedly asked administration officials for policy or legal recommendations on dealing with the ongoing threat of Russian interference in the midterm elections. They got none. Another example involves the National Defense Authorization Act, which primarily governs the yearly budget of the Defense Department. It requires that the secretary of defense prepare a "military cyber operation in response to malicious cyber activity carried out against the United States or a United States person by a foreign power." The secretary cannot conduct the operation without authorization, however, and President Trump has not granted it.

Congress's 2018 version of the act added two provisions dealing with "malign foreign influence operations and campaigns." One required that the president appoint someone on the National Security Council to "be responsible for the coordination of the interagency process for combating malign foreign influence operations and campaigns." The other required that person to brief Congress at least twice a year on his or her activities. President Trump signed the bill into law but indicated he would not comply with the requirements, citing executive privilege. He'd done the same the previous year, when Congress had conditioned certain funding on the president's developing and reporting to Congress on "a national policy for the United States relating to cyberspace, cybersecurity, and cyber warfare." Even as he signed it into law, President Trump indicated that he would not comply with it, saying he "strongly object[ed]" to it.

In addition, the president has failed to take care that a host of other laws be properly enforced and executed, from computer crime and anti-hacking provisions (18 U.S.C. § 1030, 2701), to economic espionage laws (18 U.S.C. § 1831), to laws barring campaign contributions or donations by foreign nationals (52 U.S.C. § 30121).

The foregoing describes a pattern of behavior—the wholesale abandonment of a core presidential duty. More than a year and a half into his administration, President Trump has reacted to the Russian attacks of 2016 and the continuing attacks with a unique blend of appeasement, ineptitude, inaction, efforts to undermine others' attempts to counter the assault—and with public deception.

RUSSIAN INTERFERENCE HAS NOT STOPPED

In August 2018, Facebook found a new Russia-based influence operation of more than 30 fake accounts, with at least 9,500 posts and 150 ads for an audience of 290,000 followers. This new operation tried to help arrange both a white supremacist rally in Washington, DC, and counterprotests to the rally. It had already organized more than twenty-five events. A Russia-backed website that had previously attempted to start a June rally in front of the White House was linked to Facebook and Twitter accounts and had also posted videos on a YouTube account. A report from McClatchy publications indicated that, as with almost all the Russia-backed social media operations, it carried content intended to "foment racial division, harden feelings over immigration, gun control and police brutality, and undermine social cohesion."

"After Election Day, the Russian government stepped on the gas," John Kelly, the CEO of Graphika, a social media intelligence firm, told National Public Radio. "Today the automated accounts of the far left and far right extremes of the American political spectrum produce as many as 25–30 times the number of messages per day on average as genuine political accounts across the mainstream. The extremes are screaming while the majority whispers."

In the past year, Russian bots flooded Twitter with hashtags and tweets designed to magnify extreme opinions or spread fake stories. Russian attacks started after mass shootings in 2017 in Las Vegas and Texas; after NFL players began taking a knee during the national anthem to protest treatment of African Americans; after Senator Al Franken was accused of sexual misconduct and subsequently resigned; after seventeen people were killed in a Parkland, Florida, high school in February 2018. Throughout, the Russia-backed trolls have also flooded Twitter with messages discrediting the investigation led by special counsel Robert Mueller.

Russia is also continuing to attack politicians. Microsoft reported in the summer of 2018 that it had shut down a "sophisticated" effort to hack the email accounts of three candidates for Congress. Senators Claire McCaskill of Missouri and Jeanne Shaheen of New Hampshire, both Democrats, later disclosed that their offices were two of the three targets. In August 2018, Microsoft reported new Russian hacking efforts, this time aimed at the Senate and at Republican think tanks.

In March 2018, the Department of Homeland Security and the FBI reported that the Russian government cyber targeted and infiltrated critical infrastructure, including "energy, nuclear, commercial facilities, water, aviation, and critical manufacturing sectors." It went on to detail "a multi-stage intrusion campaign by Russian government cyber actors who targeted small commercial facilities' networks where they staged malware, conducted spear phishing, and gained remote access into energy sector networks. After obtaining access, the Russian government cyber actors conducted network reconnaissance, moved laterally, and collected information pertaining to Industrial Control Systems."

In the summer of 2018, the DHS provided more details about these efforts made in 2017–18. It said that Russia's military intelligence had gained access to the control rooms of power plants throughout the nation, enabling it to take over parts of the power grid if it wanted to. According to sources interviewed by the *New York Times,* the Department of Homeland Security understated the threat: "[I]t is possible that Russian hackers are holding their fire until closer to Election Day in November."

And as with the 2016 Russian efforts, President Trump has denied the assaults. When asked in July 2018 by a reporter whether Russia was "still targeting the US," President Trump responded: "No." The White House quickly attempted to backtrack, explaining that his "no" was his way of declining to answer the question—echoing his would/wouldn't the day after Helsinki. At best, he is refusing to discuss or provide a clear message about ongoing cyberassaults. At worst, he is deliberately and repeatedly deceiving the American people about a major danger to our country from a foreign power.

His own intelligence heads, however, have warned us about the current assaults. "I believe that President Putin has clearly come to the conclusion that there's little price to pay and that therefore, 'I can continue this activity,'" former NSA head Rogers told Congress in February 2018.

Director of National Intelligence Dan Coats told the Senate Intelligence Committee in February 2018: "Frankly, the US is under attack. . . . There should be no doubt that Russia perceives its past efforts as successful and views the 2018 US midterm elections as a potential target for Russian influence operations." On July 13, 2018, Coats stepped up his warnings: "It was in the months prior to September 2001 when, according to then-CIA Director George Tenet, the system was blinking red. And here we are nearly two decades later, and I'm here to say the warning lights are blinking red again. Today, the digital infrastructure that serves this country is literally under attack."

Despite these warnings and the history of past Russian attacks, the president has been disturbingly passive and deceptive about them.

THE CASE FOR IMPEACHMENT

The first article of impeachment against Richard Nixon charged him with "making false or misleading public statements for the purpose of deceiving the American people"—his claims that a full investigation of the Watergate cover-up had taken place and that no one in the White House was involved. The deceptions were part of Nixon's effort to cover up the burglary—and keep his responsibility for it hidden—and to remove pressure for a fuller investigation.

President Trump's deceptions are designed to cover up or muddy the fact of Russia's election interference and thereby remove pressure for him to act against Russia.

President Nixon's use of presidential powers to effectuate a cover-up of the Watergate break-in, to wiretap journalists, to direct audits of an enemies list of his political opponents, and to carry out other nefarious activities was motivated by personal and political goals that had nothing to do with the welfare of the country. In impeding lawful investigations into the break-in, he aimed, initially, to ensure his reelection in 1972 and, afterward, to avoid his own or his aides' prosecution. This was central to the second article of impeachment.

President Trump's refusal to acknowledge Russian interference and develop a feasible plan to protect our electoral system has nothing to do with our country's well-being. He has never articulated any reason for refusing to act that relates to America's interests. In fact, some on his staff suggest he is unable in his mind to separate Russian interference from the legitimacy of his election. There are other possible explanations for his passivity: Perhaps Russia has some hold over him, such as the salacious *kompromat* described in the so-called Steele dossier, compiled in 2016 by Christopher Steele, former head of the Russia desk for the British foreign intelligence agency MI6. (Putin was careful at Helsinki to leave that possibility open.) Is President Trump laying the groundwork for expanded business activities in Russia after his presidency ends? Or is he simply grateful for Russia's help in the 2016 presidential election and hoping to receive it again in the elections of 2018 and 2020? All of these would be impermissible rationales—particularly given the grave consequences of his inaction—and could make President Trump liable for impeachment.

His inaction violates the "take care" clause of the Constitution, his oath of office, and his responsibilities as commander in chief to protect our country from attack by a foreign power eager to exercise some deleterious influence over our political system. We are nearing another federal election and face ongoing Russian efforts to destabilize our democracy without a significant response by our president. In the absence of protection against manipulation, the 2018 results at the polls, particularly in close races, may be easily and successfully challenged, causing untold disruption, even chaos.

The danger cannot be overstated: Russia assaulted our election machinery and manipulated public opinion through social media to sow disruption and turmoil. Its actions may have affected the outcome of the 2016 elections. President Trump has been apprised of this by cabinet-level intelligence officers, many of his choosing, and has failed to address the attacks by developing a comprehensive plan that could rally the country behind him. President Trump's refusal to act endangers the people's right to free elections, a foundation of our democracy; is a "great and dangerous offense"; and subverts the Constitution. Impeachment is the remedy our Constitution provides for such misdeeds.

4

Preventing, Obstructing, Impeding, and Abusing the Administration of Justice

The first article of impeachment voted against President Richard Nixon charged him with impeding and obstructing the administration of justice. Simply stated, Article I dealt with Nixon's cover-up of the Watergate break-in. It specified the many different actions he took to interfere with the criminal justice system and congressional inquiries in order to ensure his reelection, and then to protect his aides and himself from prosecution and prison. Aside from other non-Watergate matters, Article II charged Nixon with abusing the powers of his office when he interfered with the several investigations to cover up the break-in and protect the guilty, including himself.

A decidedly bipartisan House Judiciary Committee approved the two articles by slightly more than a two-thirds majority, deeply troubled by a president who had used his office to undermine the rule of law, under which individuals, regardless of status or connection, are held accountable for their crimes or misdeeds. Concluding that President Nixon had "acted in a manner contrary to his trust as President and subversive of constitutional government, to the great prejudice of the cause of law and justice, and to the manifest injury of the people of the United States," it found his conduct "warrants impeachment and trial, and removal from office."

Our nation takes tampering with or thwarting the institutions of justice very seriously. The Declaration of Independence asserted that George III "obstructed the Administration of Justice by refusing his Assent to Laws for establishing Judiciary Powers." Moreover, it charged, he had "obstruct[ed] the Laws for Naturalization of Foreigners." This kind of obstruction was one of the reasons our nation started an armed revolution. It is also a reason to impeach a president. I would know.

When presidents take the oath of office, they promise to "faithfully exe-cute the Office of President of the United States." The Constitution requires that a president "take Care that the Laws be faithfully executed." Interference with or obstruction of the administration of justice is an assault on the faith that binds the president to the people and that makes our representative democracy possible—the faith that the president acts for the benefit of the country as a whole and not for the president's own benefit. It is an attack on a core democratic value when the tremendous power of the state is warped and corrupted for the president's personal purposes.

But instead of keeping faith, President Trump has in fact unremittingly sought to manipulate our justice system to protect himself and his family and to punish his enemies—and has persistently tried to deceive the American people about his intentions and actions.

THE INVESTIGATIONS INTO PRESIDENT TRUMP THAT HE ATTEMPTED TO OBSTRUCT OR IMPEDE

President Trump, members of his family, and a number of his close associates have been at the center of a number of criminal investigations for much of the last two years. They are personally at risk of indictment and conviction, not to mention prison sentences, and their business interests are at risk as well. So the president's incentive to use the power of his office to evade a thorough investigation and responsibility is very high.

The FBI opened its inquiry into connections between Russia and the Trump campaign four months before the 2016 election, prompted by the rev-elation that a Trump campaign foreign policy adviser, George Papadopoulos, had boasted of dirt the Russians had on Hillary Clinton to the Australian ambassador to the United Kingdom over drinks at a London bar. When stolen Democratic emails were leaked two months later, Australian officials alerted American law enforcement to the conversation, and the FBI opened its inves-tigation in July. Through the summer and fall of 2016, the FBI learned of numerous contacts between the Trump campaign, Russians, and possible Russian agents, arousing suspicion that a Russian influence operation was under way. First reported by the *New York Times* in late October 2016, the FBI inquiry continued after the election.

At roughly the same time, the FBI and the Department of Justice began pursuing an investigation into one of the Trump campaign's top national security advisers, General Michael T. Flynn. But this inquiry did not involve Russia; instead, the initial focus was on Flynn's illegal work as a paid lobbyist for Turkey.

A third investigation was launched in early 2017, this time aimed at the illegal lobbying work on behalf of pro-Russian political elements in Ukraine by former Trump campaign manager Paul Manafort.

By far the largest, most intensive investigation began on May 17, 2017, when the Department of Justice announced the appointment of special counsel Mueller "to ensure a full and thorough investigation of the Russian government's efforts to interfere in the 2016 presidential election." Mueller was appointed to this post as a result of what has been viewed as one of the most imprudent and disgraceful acts of the Trump presidency, the firing of FBI director James Comey, a move discussed later in this chapter.

Mueller was specifically charged with looking into "any links and/or coordination between the Russian government and individuals associated with the campaign of President Donald Trump; and . . . any matters that arose or may arise directly from the investigation." He also was authorized to "investigate and prosecute federal crimes committed in the course of, and with intent to interfere with, the Special Counsel's investigation, such as perjury, obstruction of justice, destruction of evidence, and intimidation of witnesses." Mueller also took over the inquiries into Flynn and Manafort.

In the close to fifteen months since the appointment, his office has secured guilty verdicts or pleas from four Trump campaign officials: Flynn, Manafort, Papadopoulos, and Rick Gates, the former deputy chairman of the Trump campaign. Two other people, Alex van der Zwaan, a former lawyer for Manafort, and Richard Pinedo, who assisted in Russian election interference, also pleaded guilty to federal crimes. Twenty-six Russians (a subset of the thirty-four previously mentioned) and three companies have also been indicted, as detailed in Chapter 3.

In 2018, two other investigations relating to President Trump were launched. In New York, federal prosecutors independent of Mueller raided the office of Michael Cohen, President Trump's sometime personal lawyer and fixer, who had also worked for the Trump Organization before the election. In August 2018, he pleaded guilty to eight federal crimes, including campaign finance violations, tax fraud, and bank fraud. Separately, the Manhattan district attorney's office announced it was looking into possible criminal violations by the Trump Organization stemming from facts uncovered in the Cohen matter, and the New York state tax authority launched a

whether the Trump Foundation had violated criminal tax law.
...ths earlier, the state's attorney general also brought a civil action against the foundation for numerous improprieties.

Like every American, President Trump is presumed innocent. He has a battery of constitutional rights available to him. He can and has hired numerous lawyers to deal with these investigations. He might even be able to use some of his reelection campaign funds to pay for them. Unlike most Americans, President Trump has additional protections. Some of his legal bills are footed by the American taxpayer. He may have the ability to assert executive privilege in some instances to keep some material from investigators and, in contrast to every other American, may even be able to avoid prosecution while in office, a possibility that two Justice Department legal memos advocate. Not satisfied with such rights and privileges to protect himself, President Trump may have impeachably abused his power by trying to block and interfere with our justice system.

How President Trump Appears to Have Prevented, Obstructed, or Impeded the Administration of Justice

President Trump's apparent interference with investigations and prosecutions concerning him began quickly after he was sworn into office. He has employed a broad range of tactics:

First, he has attempted to influence law enforcement officials and has used or threatened to use his power to hire and fire them to coerce them.

Second, he has caused a witness in a law enforcement inquiry to issue misleading statements.

Third, he has attempted to influence other witnesses or targets of the investigation through promises of pardons or by attempting to intimidate and retaliate against them.

Fourth, he has engaged in a persistent barrage of verbal attacks to discredit the investigations and the investigators and has utilized harassing techniques to damage law enforcement agencies and personnel.

Fifth, he has abused his authority to gain access to sensitive investigative documents and information relating to him.

Sixth, he has demanded DOJ investigations of political opponents to advance his narrow political agenda and divert the investigations from their central objective, and abused the powers of his presidency to retaliate in other ways against and injure people he regards as his personal or political enemies.

Interference with Law Enforcement Officials and Abuse of Power to Intimidate Officials for Personal and Corrupt Reasons

A key example of President Trump's interference is his firing of FBI director Comey. It is highly reminiscent of President Nixon's order to fire the special Watergate prosecutor for seeking damaging White House tapes. As we have seen, that firing triggered the impeachment inquiry against President Nixon.

On February 13, 2017, President Trump fired Flynn, who had moved from a role on the campaign to national security adviser, one of the most sensitive and powerful jobs in the administration, involving access to the nation's most important secrets. Flynn was fired by President Trump for purportedly lying to Vice President Mike Pence about a telephone conversation he had in late December 2016 with Sergey Kislyak, the Russian ambassador to the United States.

This was no standard-issue firing for workplace dishonesty. The call had been made public shortly after President Trump's inauguration, and rumors that Kislyak and Flynn had discussed relaxing US sanctions against Russia abounded, threatening a huge scandal days into the new presidency. Since President-elect Trump had not yet been sworn in, a promise to modify US policy would have been a grave breach of protocol, if not of the constitutional order. Worse, some asked, were Flynn's suggestions part of a payoff to Russia in thanks for its assistance to Trump in the election?

Flynn had reportedly told the vice president that the call was a simple courtesy and that he had just wished the ambassador happy holidays. It was a lie. He had in fact discussed sanctions with Kislyak—specifically, that the incoming administration might look favorably on changing them.

Flynn's exposure was far greater than just being caught in a fib. As noted above, he was already under investigation by the FBI for secretly working as a paid lobbyist for Turkey during the campaign. Flynn had told prospective White House counsel Donald McGahn II about the investigation in early January, before the inauguration. Moreover, Flynn had been questioned at the White House by the FBI. He lied to them, potentially a felony, and there were recordings to prove it: Kislyak was under surveillance by the American intelligence community. Worse yet, DOJ officials had told McGahn multiple times that they were worried that Flynn might be vulnerable to blackmail from Russia over the Kislyak call: the Russians knew he was lying to the vice president, the public, and the press and could threaten to expose his lies. Flynn nevertheless stayed in office for eighteen days; President Trump fired him on February 13 only after word of the blackmail potential was leaked to the *Washington Post.*

At the time, President Trump probably knew he was at risk in the Flynn matter. Not only had he hired a national security adviser who had been sur-reptitiously on the payroll of Turkey, who was being investigated by the Justice Department for it, and who had lied to the vice president and the FBI, but he had kept Flynn in office after being alerted Flynn could be black-mailed. The peril may even have extended beyond the scandal it brought his White House. Flynn may have had intimate, and damaging, knowledge of the campaign's activities in 2016, potentially including overtures, conversa-tions, or coordination with Russian actors. In December 2015, he was in Russia on a paid trip and was seated beside President Putin at a dinner; across from the two men was Green Party presidential candidate Jill Stein, later investigated by the Senate Intelligence Committee for possible "collu-sion with the Russians." The occasion for the dinner was the tenth anniver-sary of *RT*, the TV network.

The day after Flynn's dismissal, President Trump met in the Oval Office with James Comey, Attorney General Jeff Sessions, and others. According to Comey, President Trump asked the others to leave in order to talk privately with him. President Trump allegedly told Comey that Flynn did nothing wrong in speaking to the Russian ambassador and added: "I hope you can see your way clear to letting this go, to letting Flynn go. He's a good guy. I hope you can let this go." Comey later testified before the Senate Intelligence Committee that he took President Trump's remarks "as a direction." President Trump's directive was not about an idle possibility. Just before the Oval Office meeting, then-Chief of Staff Reince Priebus and McGahn had told President Trump that Flynn was under investigation by the FBI, according to a memorandum prepared by McGahn. The next day, Priebus called Comey and FBI deputy director Andrew McCabe and asked them to rebut press stories about Trump campaign ties to Russia and possibly to discuss what the FBI knew of those connections.

The request for leniency with Flynn came less than three weeks after President Trump and Comey had shared a private dinner at the White

House, at which, according to Comey, President Trump asked whether he was planning to stay on. President Trump then twice asked for a pledge of loyalty. Comey replied that he would provide honesty.

On March 20, 2017, Comey testified before the House Intelligence Committee and confirmed that the Department of Justice was investigating Russia's interference in the election and its possible ties to the Trump campaign. Moreover, he rebutted President Trump's claims, made earlier that month, that President Barack Obama had wiretapped Trump. On March 30, President Trump called Comey, asking him to "lift the cloud" of the investigation. Comey's contemporaneous memos of the call show that President Trump was fixated on his personal involvement in the investigation. He told Comey he had nothing to do with Russia, that he was not involved with hookers in Russia, and that he was suing Christopher Steele, author of a report (the Steele dossier) provided to the FBI detailing possible Trump-Russia connections. (He did not sue Steele.) Twelve days later, President Trump called Comey, again asking him to lift the cloud, "because I have been very loyal to you, very loyal; we had that thing you know," according to Comey's memo. Comey and senior FBI staff listening to the call interpreted President Trump's language as "a veiled threat." It was the last time President Trump and Comey spoke.

On May 3, 2017, Comey testified before the Senate Judiciary Committee. He again confirmed the Russia investigation and said that he felt "mildly nauseous" to think that his public comments about the Clinton email investigation had affected the outcome of the election. President Trump fired Comey six days later. Publicly, at first, President Trump claimed that Comey was fired for mishandling the FBI investigation into Hillary Clinton's use of a private email server while she was secretary of state. The president pointed to a memorandum he had asked the deputy attorney general, Rod Rosenstein, to prepare on the issue. The day after Comey's firing, however, President Trump met privately with Russian ambassador Kislyak and Russian foreign minister Sergey V. Lavrov in the Oval Office, where he is reported to have told the two: "I just fired the head of the F.B.I. He was crazy, a real nut job," according to a leaked report of the meeting. "I faced great pressure because of Russia. That's taken off," the president added. He also reportedly assured the two that he was not under investigation.

Then, on May 11, he told Lester Holt that when he fired Comey, "this Russia thing" was on his mind. Although he had asked Sessions and Rosenstein to tell him what the "case" against Comey was, he told Holt he was going to fire Comey "regardless of the recommendation [from Rosenstein]. . . . And in fact when I decided to do it, I said to myself, I said you know, this Russia thing with Trump and Russia is a made-up story."

As the impeachment articles against Nixon make clear, a president who fires the person heading the investigation for self-protection purposes likely commits an impeachable offense.

Other Interference

James Comey is the most prominent but not the only senior law enforcement officer President Trump has attempted to pressure, coerce, or control regarding the Russia investigations. Shortly after Comey's March 20, 2017, testimony, President Trump once again cleared the Oval Office after a meeting to have a private conversation with people about the Russia investigation. This time, he kept Director of National Intelligence Dan Coats and Mike Pompeo, then CIA director, in the room. He asked Coats to persuade Comey to back off Flynn. A few days later, President Trump called Coats and National Security Administration Director Admiral Mike Rogers to urge them to deny the existence of any evidence of collusion during the 2016 election. Both reportedly regarded the request as inappropriate.

Some of President Trump's most relentless efforts to influence the Russia investigations focused on the attorney general of the United States, the nation's top law enforcement officer. On March 2, 2017, Jeff Sessions recused himself from investigations relating to Russia and the 2016 campaign. He did so after consulting with Justice Department ethics officials and after revelations that he had had several meetings with Russians that he had not disclosed to the Senate during testimony on the matter. The decision, which President Trump knew of beforehand, took supervision of the various Russia probes out of the hands of a man the president regarded as a loyalist. Before the decision was finalized, President Trump directed his White House counsel to tell Sessions not to recuse himself, and shortly after the recusal, at a dinner at Mar-a-Lago, he reportedly berated Sessions for recusing himself and asked him to reverse the decision. Sessions refused.

On May 17, 2017, upon learning of Mueller's appointment, made by Deputy Attorney General Rosenstein in light of Sessions's recusal, President Trump accused Sessions of "disloyalty" for failing to stay in charge of the Russia investigation. He attacked Sessions repeatedly, until Sessions submitted his resignation, which President Trump rejected. Many believed that

President Trump wanted to force Sessions to resign so that he could replace him with someone who would not have to recuse himself and who would fire special counsel Robert Mueller. Press reports indicate President Trump changed his mind and kept Sessions on only after he realized that the Senate would turn on him if Sessions were forced out.

Reince Priebus, President Trump's former chief of staff, explained to ABC News in June 2017, "He feels like that [Sessions's recusal] was a—the first sin, the original sin, and he feels slighted by it. . . . He doesn't like it, and he's not going to let it go." President Trump also reportedly told Priebus in late July to obtain Sessions's resignation.

The attacks against Sessions continued in 2018. In February, the president publicly scolded Sessions for a decision to refer allegations of possible FBI misconduct relating to the Russia investigation to an internal review process rather than a criminal prosecutor. President Trump objected; he wanted FBI agents criminally prosecuted and complained that the internal process was led by an Obama-era appointee. "DISGRACEFUL," he tweeted. Sessions responded in a statement: "As long as I am the Attorney General, I will continue to discharge my duties with integrity and honor, and this Department will continue to do its work in a fair and impartial manner according to the law and Constitution." The implications are clear: Sessions saw the president's relentless attacks as an effort to push him to act in an unfair and biased manner.

President Trump's attacks escalated in August 2018 as the Manafort trial began. On the third day of the trial, he began telling his attorney general to shut down the Mueller inquiry. He tweeted: "This is a terrible situation and Attorney General Jeff Sessions should stop this Rigged Witch Hunt right now, before it continues to stain our country any further."

Shortly after a jury convicted Manafort of eight crimes and after Cohen pleaded guilty to eight crimes, President Trump publicly threatened that he might simply take over the investigation himself. In an interview with Reuters, he said: "I've decided to stay out. Now I don't have to stay out. I can go in, and I could do whatever—I could run it if I want. But I decided to stay out," he said. "I'm totally allowed to be involved if I wanted to be. So far, I haven't chosen to be involved. I'll stay out."

President Trump then turned to Sessions, in an interview with *Fox & Friends*, indicating that personal loyalty, or its lack, was the ultimate criterion for hiring or firing the attorney general. When asked whether he was going to fire Sessions, President Trump replied: "Even my enemies say that

Jeff Sessions should have told you that he was going to recuse himself and then you wouldn't have put him in. He took the job and then he said, 'I'm going to recuse myself.' I said, 'What kind of a man is this?' And by the way, he was on the campaign. You know, the only reason I gave him the job is because I felt loyalty. He was an original supporter."

Hours after the interview aired, Sessions issued a statement: "While I am Attorney General, the actions of the Department of Justice will not be improperly influenced by political considerations." As with the February 2018 statement, the clear implication is that the attorney general felt the president was attempting to interfere wrongfully and politically with the administration of justice.

Sessions has not been the only high-ranking DOJ target of the president's vitriol. Deputy Attorney General Rod Rosenstein, who is overseeing the Russia investigation, has faced the president's ire as well. And according to press reports, Mueller, too, has faced the threat of termination. In June 2017, President Trump reportedly ordered Mueller's firing, a directive thwarted only when White House counsel McGahn threatened to resign. President Trump reportedly gave a similar order in December 2017, when word spread that Mueller had subpoenaed records from one of the president's top bankers, Deutsche Bank, which has provided financing for at least three of the Trump Organization's largest properties. Deutsche Bank would have been of particular interest to Mueller, because it was in the midst of an investigation into a $10 billion Russian money-laundering scheme involving its Moscow, New York, and London branches; the bank eventually agreed to pay roughly $630 million in penalties.

President Trump also has apparently tried to influence more than just Department of Justice proceedings. During the summer of 2017, he reportedly complained to Senate majority leader Mitch McConnell in a private phone call that he was failing to shield him from the Senate inquiry into Russian collusion with the Trump campaign. President Trump also called Senator Richard Burr, chair of the Senate Intelligence Committee, and told him it was time to move on with respect to the committee's Russia investigation. President Trump called other members of that committee and other senators, urging them to pressure Burr to end the committee's inquiry. At that point, according to *Newsweek*, President Trump had approached seven officials with a request either to speed up or end the Russian investigations.

Causing a Witness to a Law Enforcement Inquiry to Issue Misleading Statements

A pivotal moment under investigation by the special counsel is the June 2016 meeting at Trump Tower in New York where Donald Trump Jr., campaign manager Manafort, and the president's son-in-law, Jared Kushner, met with Natalia Veselnitskaya and other people she brought along. Veselnitskaya, a Russian lawyer, has acknowledged that she was an informant for a high-level Russian official—likely its prosecutor general, the country's chief legal officer.

The meeting was set up via emails between Trump Jr. and a British music publicist with ties to a Russian oligarch, Aras Agalarov, who had partnered with Trump in the Miss Universe pageant in 2013, held in Moscow, and was also reportedly close to Putin. The email chain indicated that participants, at least four of them Russian nationals, would "provide the Trump campaign with some official documents and information that would incriminate Hillary and her dealings with Russia and would be very useful to your father." It also mentioned that the information was "part of Russia and its government's support for Mr. Trump." In agreeing to the meeting, Trump Jr. wrote: "[I]f it's what you say I love it.

Many months later, after news of the meeting broke in 2017, President Trump coordinated with his son to craft a story about it. On July 8, as he was flying on *Air Force One* to the United States after a G20 meeting of heads of state (including a private, nearly hour-long one-on-one with Putin with no US translator or aide present), President Trump personally dictated a statement to the *New York Times* for his son. Its essence was that the meeting had nothing to do with Russian interference in the elections: "We primarily discussed a program about the adoption of Russian children that was active and popular with American families years ago and was since ended by the Russian government, but it was not a campaign issue at the time and there was no follow up." After the email chain setting up the meeting was disclosed a day later, Trump Jr.'s explanation shifted. In a second statement, he acknowledged that it had been set up to obtain negative information about Clinton, but, he emphasized, in the end, the meeting was really about adoptions. Trump Jr. has stuck to the topline narrative devised by his father in that statement. In sworn testimony to the Senate Judiciary Committee in September 2017, he stressed repeatedly that the meeting was focused on adoptions.

President Trump's explanation of his involvement in crafting his son's statement has also moved about. In July 2017, one of his lawyers indicated that President Trump was not involved at all. In August 2017, his press secretary said he "weighed in" on but did not "dictate" the statement. Finally, a January 2018 memorandum sent by President Trump's lawyers to Mueller confirmed that Trump was the author of the statement. "[T]he President dictated a short but accurate response," the memo says. The statement drafted by President Trump about adoptions was not accurate; it was a story, a clear attempt to reframe and obfuscate the real purpose of the Trump Tower meeting, which was to get dirt on Hillary Clinton.

President Trump finally slipped eight months later, admitting the real purpose of the Trump Tower meeting in an August 5, 2018, tweet: "This was a meeting to get information on an opponent, totally legal and done all the time in politics—and it went nowhere . . . ." His story shifted again later in August in a statement to the *Washington Post*: "nothing happened after the meeting concluded." He then qualified his statement with the lawyerly "to the best of my knowledge."

The president's involvement in influencing a key witness's recollection of a critical event could form a basis for impeachment under the precedent established in the first article of impeachment against Nixon; its third element dealt with "[a]pproving, condoning, acquiescing in, and counselling witnesses with respect to the giving of false or misleading statements to lawfully authorized investigative officers and employees of the United States."

Though more facts are needed to flesh out a charge against President Trump for the attempt to influence a witness, as a participant in the Nixon impeachment inquiry, I believe that it also falls under the charge of "deceiving the people of the United States." In the impeachment inquiry, one of Nixon's main deceptions involved his false claims that the Watergate cover-up had been fully investigated by John Dean, his White House counsel—who, according to Nixon, found that no one in the White House was responsible. The Dean "investigation" was a fraud concocted by President Nixon. Similarly, the memo dictated by President Trump for his son, disguising the true intent of the Trump Tower meeting, appears to be a fraud, with the goal of hiding the truth from the American public.

Interference by Suggestions of Presidential Pardons

President Nixon authorized offers of pardon to the burglars to keep them quiet. No pardons were issued, but the offers became one of the grounds for the Judiciary Committee's impeachment vote. Although the Constitution grants the president broad pardon powers, a president who uses them to impede a criminal investigation by buying silence and discouraging coopera-tion with a federal investigation/prosecution commits an impeachable offense. This precedent is crystal clear. It is indelibly imprinted on my memory, because the pardon offers were part of John Dean's "cancer on the presidency" conver-sation in which he warned the former president about the cover-up. Watergate should have given President Trump pause, but apparently it did not.

In fact, the president has disregarded the Watergate precedent, tweeting on July 22, 2017, that he has "complete power to pardon." The tweet, accord-ing to the *New York Times,* may have been in response to a *Washington Post* report that the president had discussed pardons, as well as efforts to limit and "stymie" the Mueller investigation, with his advisers.

President Trump's formulation of his pardon power is incorrect. It does not, for example, extend to crimes under state law—nor, in my opinion, to a self-pardon. The evidence, however, is not conclusive yet with respect to whether President Trump has clearly abused the pardon power in Watergate fashion, although he may well have. On December 15, 2017, after his former national security adviser was indicted and questions were raised in the press about whether he would pardon Flynn and others, including himself, President Trump declared that he wasn't considering pardons "at that time"—leaving the door open. Indeed, months earlier, in March 2017, President Trump had suggested as much when he tweeted: "Mike Flynn should ask for immunity in that this is a witch hunt (excuse for big election loss), by media & Dems, of historic proportion!" The president's comments appear to be signals to Flynn and possibly others not to talk too much to Mueller's investigators in the hope of getting a pardon down the road. Further investigation is needed to uncover what the president may have meant by these comments and whether he told others about any plans to pardon Flynn.

In addition, it has been widely reported that John Dowd, President Trump's former lawyer handling the Mueller investigation, discussed presi-dential pardons in the summer of 2017 with lawyers for Flynn and Manafort. Dowd has refused to comment on the reports. An investigation is needed to ascertain whether Dowd had these conversations, and if so, what was said, and whether Dowd was acting at President Trump's behest and what, if any, instructions he received from President Trump.

President Trump may again have flirted with pardoning a key witness. After Manafort's August 2018 conviction by a Virginia jury, and with a second criminal trial looming, President Trump may have tried to signal to him by praising him. Manafort, the president tweeted, was "brave" for refusing to "break" under pressure. "I feel badly for Paul Manafort, I must tell you." Asked by a Fox reporter whether he would pardon Manafort, the president replied: "I have great respect for what he has done in terms of what he has gone through. . . ."—leaving the door to a pardon still open. In the same interview, President Trump chastised "flippers," or people who agree to testify against another person. "It's called flipping and it almost ought to be illegal," Trump said. "I know all about flipping, 30, 40 years I have been watching flippers. Everything is wonderful and then they get 10 years in jail and they flip on whoever the next highest one is or as high as you can go." When the *Washington Post* reported that President Trump had asked his legal team about pardoning Manafort, the White House press secretary, apparently further opening the door to a pardon, explained that "the president has not made a decision on pardoning Paul Manafort or anyone else."

Despite these signs of a possible pardon, both Flynn and Manafort have pleaded guilty to crimes and agreed to cooperate with the Mueller probe.

While more facts are needed to flesh out possible charges, if President Trump authorized pardon offers in return for non-cooperation with Mueller— or even suggested the possibility in tweets or comments to the media—they could be impeachable offenses. Even if he did not succeed in influencing Flynn and Manafort, the very fact that he tried to would be impeachable. Under the ninth part of Article I against President Nixon, "Endeavouring to cause prospective defendants, and individuals duly tried and convicted, to expect favoured treatment and consideration in return for their silence or false testimony, or rewarding individuals for their silence and false testimony" is an impeachable offense.

President Trump's attacking "flipping" or cooperation with a prosecutor may be another abuse of his office. Discouraging a witness from talking to a prosecutor may be improper, if not criminal, for a civilian; but for a president, required to take care that the laws be faithfully executed, it may be a high crime and misdemeanor. The lessons of Watergate resound here: presidents cannot—without becoming liable to impeachment—use the power of the presidency to interfere with an investigation to shield themselves from criminal prosecution.

Persistent Efforts to Undermine the Investigation, Investigators, and Witnesses

Thus far, the Mueller investigation has indicted thirty-four people, more than two dozen of whom were Russian operatives, and three companies, as we have seen. It has procured five guilty pleas. So it seems absurd and outrageous to characterize the investigations as a witch hunt, wild goose chase, or hoax. Nonetheless, President Trump has repeatedly belittled the investigation into Russian election interference in this way. In the two-month period between April 1 and May 31, 2018, he attacked the FBI, Comey, Mueller, the Russia "witch hunt," and the "deep state" more than fifty times. He called the Russia investigation a "witch hunt" forty-four times just in June and July 2018. After the Parkland school massacre, he made the outlandish claim that the FBI had caused the deaths of innocent Americans, mostly children, by "spending too much time trying to prove Russian collusion with the Trump campaign—there is no collusion. Get back to the basics."

This illustrates a grave risk posed to the rule of law by President Trump's astounding, unprincipled, and unfounded attacks on the integrity of federal law enforcement: if he were to convince millions of Americans that the FBI is politically biased, consequences could range from undermining public willingness to cooperate with the FBI to destroying the credibility of FBI agents, making it harder for the government to win convictions in ordinary, nonpolitical cases.

These attacks may also serve to poison the minds of a jury selected to sit on any of the trials that may arise from the many indictments Mueller has brought.

President Trump has relentlessly attacked Comey and top officials at the FBI who might serve as witnesses to his efforts to interfere in the Russia investigation. He has also denigrated the FBI, the CIA, Mueller, and the members of his team by charging them with alleged conflicts of interest, which the Justice Department itself has refuted. The president may well have taken these attacks to Nixonian levels on at least four occasions:

1. In June 2017, *Foreign Policy* reported that President Trump "pressed senior aides . . . to devise and carry out a campaign to discredit

senior FBI officials after learning that those specific employees were likely to be witnesses against him as part of special counsel Robert Mueller's investigation." If true, using the power of his office to discredit potential witnesses against him can easily form a basis for impeachment. It is a great and dangerous offense for presidents to use the powers of the presidency to block or discredit a potential case against them—the gravamen of the first two articles of impeachment against Nixon.

2. In September 2017, President Trump sent a letter to Deputy Attorney General Rosenstein requesting a federal grand jury investigation of Comey, a key witness to his apparent obstruction of the Russia investigation.

3. In March 2018, following the firing of FBI Deputy Director Andrew McCabe, President Trump tweeted: "Andrew McCabe FIRED, a great day for the hard working men and women of the FBI. . . . He knew all about the lies and corruption going on at the highest levels of the FBI!" Earlier in 2018, at President Trump's behest, Sessions had pressured FBI Director Christopher Wray to fire McCabe. Wray threatened to resign if his deputy were removed. Ultimately, Sessions did fire McCabe, reportedly to curry favor with the president, after a critical report by the inspector general regarding McCabe's alleged lack of candor about a leak to the press in 2016. The firing could amount to retaliation against a prospective witness, a possible crime and/or impeachable offense.

    McCabe may have been in President Trump's crosshairs because he was a witness to several of Comey's calls with the president. In an introductory meeting with McCabe, who was then acting FBI director, President Trump reportedly asked about how he had voted in the 2016 election and attacked McCabe's s wife, who had run for office in Virginia as a Democrat and received funds from a Clinton ally. Trump denied having ever asked the question about how he'd voted and downplayed its significance by saying it wasn't "a big deal." Of course, dealing with subordinates on the basis of their political views or affiliations or those of their spouses may be an abuse of power—and may in this case constitute another part of the president's effort to signal that he wants political loyalty from governmental agencies that need to do their work on a nonpartisan and professional basis. This calls to mind Nixon's Enemies List, where penalizing people for their political views created impeachment liability.

These attacks, as well as others by the president, may have been intended to (and did in fact) send a signal to senior law enforcement officials that their jobs were at risk if they defied him or weren't "loyal." The harmful impact of such intimidation on professional law enforcement can be incalculable. Just asking the question shows the cloud that now hovers over the FBI, undermining the public's confidence in its impartiality and professionalism and possibly its willingness to cooperate with it and accept the honesty of its agents.

4. In August 2018, President Trump threatened to use his unilateral authority to revoke security clearances to retaliate against people who he felt were hostile to him. He revoked the security clearance of former CIA director John Brennan and indicated that he was still considering whether to withdraw the clearances of at least one other probable witness in the Mueller inquiry, former acting attorney general Sally Q. Yates, who had briefed the White House about Flynn's blackmail vulnerability.

In his zeal to attack the Mueller investigation, President Trump was partly responsible for the outing of an FBI Confidential Human Source. By May 2018, at the latest, the president learned that the FBI had used a confidential informant in 2016 to speak with three Trump campaign employees regarding Russian efforts to infiltrate the campaign. President Trump learned of the informant's existence as members of the House Intelligence Committee were attempting to gain access to Justice Department material on that informant. Simultaneously, several conservative news outlets began speculating about the informant's existence and identity. The Justice Department tried vigorously to protect the informant's identity, but, rather than protecting an American intelligence source, President Trump confirmed his existence by tweet. He branded the intelligence effort "Spygate." Shortly after President Trump gave the signal that the informant was fair game, his identity was blown. Presidents who misuse their powers to out an intelligence agent— with all the negative consequences for US intelligence activities that protect our country from hostile powers—in order to exonerate themselves from criminal or other personal legal liability may commit an impeachable offense, as the Nixon precedent in Watergate shows. Presidential powers are to be used for the benefit of the country, not for avoiding prosecution or other issues of personal liability.

In a CNN interview, President Trump's lawyer Rudy Giuliani acknowledged that President Trump did this (and made attacks on law enforcement) for public relations purposes and to lay the groundwork for discrediting any impeachment inquiry:

> Of course, we have to do it [be aggressive in these attacks] in defending the president. We are defending—to a large extent, remember . . . we are defending here, it is for public opinion, because eventually the decision here is going to be impeach, not impeach. Members of Congress, Democrat and Republican, are going to be informed a lot by their constituents. So, our jury is the American— as it should be—is the American people. And the American people, yes, are . . . Republicans, largely, independents, pretty substantially, and even some Democrats now question the legitimacy of [the Mueller investigation].

This echoes President Nixon's strategy after the Watergate burglary became public. According to the notes of his aide H. R. Haldeman, President Nixon called for a "PR offensive to top this. . . . We should be on the attack for diversion."

Spygate was not the first time that President Trump had caused the harmful release of sensitive law enforcement material for personal public relations purposes. In February 2018, he declassified a report prepared by the Republican majority staff of the House Permanent Select Committee on Intelligence (the Nunes memo). Both the Department of Justice and the FBI strongly opposed the declassification, because it would compromise sources and methods and was misleading.

In January 2018, President Trump had met with Deputy Attorney General Rosenstein, who had requested the meeting to prevent the declassification of the Nunes memo. President Trump reportedly asked Rosenstein where the Russia investigation "was headed." In addition, President Trump asked Rosenstein whether he was "on my team"—that is, loyal—much as he had with Comey. According to CNN, Rosenstein "demurred" on the direction of the investigation and answered: "Of course, we're all on your team,

Mr. President." After the meeting, President Trump, ignoring Rosenstein's advice on the matter, declassified the Nunes memo.

The Nunes memo concerned a ruling by the Foreign Intelligence Surveillance Act (FISA) court, which oversees requests by the United States Government to conduct surveillance for foreign intelligence purposes. In 2016, the court had approved an FBI and Justice Department request for a warrant to surveil Carter Page, a former foreign policy adviser to the Trump campaign believed to be a target of Russian recruitment efforts. The Republican majority of the House Intelligence Committee argued that the FBI and the Justice Department had failed to advise the FISA court that the Steele dossier, one of the predicates for the surveillance request, had been paid for by the Hillary Clinton campaign and the DNC. The Democratic minority of the House Permanent Select Committee on Intelligence released its side of the story, showing that the investigation into the Trump campaign's possible collusion with Russia had begun weeks *before* the Steele dossier surfaced, and that the FISA court had in fact been notified that the dossier had been paid for by a party interested in opposition research on candidate Trump. The Nunes memo, which reflected the Republican majority's position, caused President Trump to claim that it vindicated him. But, of course, that was not the case—and the Russia interference investigation continues. Providing false information to the American people to distract from and to cover up the significance of a serious criminal investigation may be an impeachable offense, as it was in the Nixon case.

In sum, President Trump caused the release of a one-sided and misleading memo on a complex issue to undermine the credibility of two government agencies in a counterintelligence matter before the courts, seemingly for the purpose of securing personal exoneration and not to benefit the country.

As with similar actions by President Nixon, President Trump's attacks and actions regarding the investigation of Russian election interference appear to have been made for no apparent reason other than to protect himself from liability. The Nunes memo, like the Dean investigation, appears to have been a red herring—an effort to distract from the underlying seriousness of the investigation and to create a false exoneration. Under the Nixon precedent, Trump's pressing for the release of the Nunes memo may be an impeachable offense both as an abuse of power and as an effort to impede an investigation.

Improperly Seeking Information
About the Investigation into Himself

As part of the Watergate cover-up, Nixon met with the assistant attorney general in charge of the Criminal Division, Henry E. Petersen, and asked for detailed information of the Watergate investigation. Whether because he was intimidated or flattered, Petersen gave Nixon the information he asked for, which Nixon in turn provided to former top aides to help them try to avoid criminal prosecution. His acts in seeking and misusing the information in order to obstruct the Watergate investigation formed one of the grounds for the Judiciary Committee's impeachment vote.

It is worth noting that a similar pumping approach was made by President Trump to Deputy Attorney General Rosenstein, who reportedly rebuffed it, as discussed previously. The approach itself, coupled with the question about whether he was on the president's "team," may be an abuse of power and an effort to impede an investigation. More information would be needed about exactly what transpired.

President Trump appears improperly to have tried to use the House Intelligence Committee as a back door to obtain information about the investigation. When the committee was seeking documents relating to the scope of Mueller's investigation in April, the Justice Department resisted. President Trump attacked the decision, tweeting: "So sad that the Department of 'Justice' and the FBI are slow walking, or even not giving, the unredacted documents requested by Congress. An embarrassment to our country!" Then, in May, the committee began seeking documents relating to yet another confidential informant who had met with members of the Trump campaign. Again, the Justice Department resisted. This time, in addition to tweeting his disapproval of the Justice Department's stance, President Trump demanded that Rosenstein, Wray, and Coats come to the White House to discuss the matter. After meeting with President Trump, they agreed to give the documents to members of Congress.

Initially, only the Republicans were to receive the documents, but after significant pushback, it was agreed that they would be released to a bipartisan group of members. Justice Department leadership arrived on Capitol Hill to provide the classified documents and a classified briefing, accompanied by White House chief of staff John Kelly and Emmet Flood, White House counsel for the Russia investigations. Both Kelly and Flood were there at President Trump's direction and instructed to relay his words. Two Democrats at the briefing warned Kelly and Flood that their attendance "could give off the appearance that the White House abused its authority to gain insight into an investigation that implicates the president." Kelly and Flood left before the material was discussed.

According to Giuliani, their attendance was a justifiable effort to obtain the information being provided to Congress. The *New York Times* quoted Giuliani: "'We are certainly entitled to know' what information the government has on the F.B.I. informant. . . . The meeting 'cuts off a long subpoena.'" At issue, as Giuliani later told the *Huffington Post*, was that the president wanted information about the informant before deciding whether to agree to be interviewed by special counsel Mueller. "We can't let our guy go in and be questioned without knowing this."

Normally, defendants in a criminal inquiry are not allowed to look into the prosecutor's files for the purpose of tailoring their defense. President Trump may have abused his authority by allegedly using the powers of his office to try to obtain access in order to determine whether to cooperate with the prosecutor and expose himself to criminal or other jeopardy. That may be an effort to impede the Russia investigation and thus may constitute a high crime and misdemeanor.

Demanding Investigations of Political Opponents for Private Political Desires

In late October and early November 2017, President Trump began publicly pushing for a new Justice Department investigation of Hillary Clinton. On October 30, the day Manafort was first indicted, President Trump tweeted: "Sorry, but this is years ago, before Paul Manafort was part of the Trump campaign. But why aren't Crooked Hillary & the Dems the focus?????"

That same week, in a November 2 interview with conservative talk-radio host Larry O'Connor, President Trump complained that as president he is not personally supposed to direct law enforcement to investigate Clinton. "The saddest thing is that because I am the president of the United States, I am not supposed to be involved with the Justice Department. I'm not supposed to be involved with the FBI. I'm not supposed to be doing the kind of things I would love to be doing, and I am very frustrated by it. I look at what's happening with the Justice Department, why aren't they going after Hillary Clinton with her emails and with her dossier and the kind of money? I don't know."

A day later, he tweeted: "Everybody is asking why the Justice Department (and FBI) isn't looking into all of the dishonesty going on with Crooked Hillary & the Dems . . . People are angry. At some point the Justice Department, and the FBI, must do what is right and proper. The American public deserves it!" Ten days later, the Justice Department confirmed in a letter to Capitol Hill that it had tasked senior prosecutors to explore whether alleged misdeeds by Hillary Clinton warranted further investigation, despite that fact that her actions were examined fully by the FBI in 2016 and found not to merit prosecution.

It will take further investigation to determine whether the Justice Department opened this new analysis in response to President Trump's political tweets and demands or came to the decision independently and as a matter of professional decision making. Regardless, President Trump's demands for a further investigation of Clinton under these circumstances may have been a misuse of power in a number of ways, because they appear to have been motivated by the "public relations" strategy highlighted by Giuliani, his lawyer, to distract attention from his misdeeds rather than for legitimate governmental objectives. Forcing the Justice Department into the role of prosecutor and investigator of a political opponent is something we associate with dictatorships and autocratic societies. In a country governed by the rule of law, prosecution may not be used for political retribution, payback, or for reasons of publicity. Prosecutions are commenced when professional prosecutors and investigators determine that there is solid basis to believe a crime has been committed.

Obstruction of the Administration of Justice

President Trump has made the breathtaking claim that a president cannot obstruct justice. In a letter his lawyers wrote in January to special counsel Mueller, they argued that "the President's actions here, by virtue of his position as the chief law enforcement officer, could neither constitutionally nor legally constitute obstruction because that would amount to him obstructing himself, and . . . he could, if he wished, terminate the inquiry, or even exercise his power to pardon if he so desired." In effect, he *is* justice and justice *is* him. The argument reeks of monarchical assertions of unfettered privilege— of *L'état, c'est moi* ("I am the state"), attributed to France's Louis XIV. In such assertions, as well as in his demands of loyalty from Comey, Sessions, and Rosenstein and his condemnation of witnesses as "flippers," he brings to mind not so much autocrats or monarchs as caricatures of organized crime leaders from movies and books.

President Trump's argument turns on two points. One, the president has the right to set law enforcement priorities. Two, the president has the right, as the nation's chief executive, to fire people. While both points may be generally true, under the present circumstances and in the present context, they cannot withstand scrutiny and reflect a view that the president is above the law.

Consider the president's right to set law enforcement priorities. No one disputes that President Trump could decide that the nation should increase its focus on counterterrorism or domestic terrorism prosecutions. He could also decide on a zero-tolerance policy toward marijuana possession. People might dispute the wisdom of his priorities, or decry the consequences of them, but no one could dispute his authority to make such decisions (or try to impeach him for it). But does anyone think that President Trump's desire to shut down the Mueller investigation is about an objective, dispassionate ordering of prosecutorial priorities? By the most aggressive accounting available, the Mueller probe has cost approximately $18 million, or a puny 0.053 percent of the Department of Justice's budget and not enough to have a material impact on the agency's ability to pursue its law enforcement priorities. The special counsel's office has approximately eighteen lawyers, including Mueller himself, and eleven FBI agents, or 0.027 percent of the 114,500 Department of Justice personnel. Numbers aside, President Trump's actions and words reveal that his interest in the Mueller probe is deeply personal. His mantra "No Collusion" refers consistently to his actions and those of his family and close associates during the 2016 campaign. He has shown interest only in the cases against people close to him and/or who might have evidence against him (Manafort, Cohen) yet has been silent about prosecutions against others (Papadopoulos, van der Zwaan).

A clear example that his efforts to shut down the Russia investigation are only about protecting him came in the spring of 2018. On April 19, Bloomberg reported that Deputy Attorney General Rosenstein had advised President Trump on April 12 that he was not a target of the Mueller or New York–based Cohen investigations. Although his attacks at that time on Mueller and Rosenstein had been so vehement they raised questions of whether he was going to fire either or both in short order, the president switched gears. He told his advisers, "[I]t's not the right time to remove either [Rosenstein or Mueller] since he's [that is, President Trump's] not a target. . . ." Note that President Trump here is basically admitting he was prepared to use the powers of the presidency to thwart normal processes of criminal accountability just to protect himself, and when it was not necessary to do so any longer, he backed off.

Indeed, he said it outright in an April 2018 tweet: "No Collusion or Obstruction (other than I fight back)." The operative word is "I," and what President Trump does not seem to fathom is that he can challenge an investigation, as anyone in this country can. What a president cannot do is "fight back" using the powers of the presidency. They are in his hands for the benefit of the people of this country, not for himself alone.

Perhaps that is why President Trump has tried to muddy the waters by asserting that the Mueller investigation is "an attack on our country." The underlying assumption, that what is not good for Donald Trump is not good for the country, hearkens back to his lawyers' assertions that he cannot break the law because he *is* the law. The president is NOT the same as the United States. It's black letter law: the case to obtain the tapes from President Nixon was entitled *United States v. Richard Nixon*, not *Nixon v. Nixon*.

Although a president has broad authority to hire and fire people in the executive branch, an improper or corrupt motive can turn a legal firing into an impeachable act, especially when coupled with a superabundance of other improper acts. President Nixon sealed his fate in late 1973 when he fired the special prosecutor, Archibald Cox, who was investigating Watergate. The firing was not the only *reason* for impeachment, but it was the trigger, sealing the decision that an impeachment inquiry was warranted by both Republicans and Democrats on the House Judiciary Committee. President Trump did not fire Comey because he thought the FBI needed new leadership, but because he thought it would alter the course of the Russia investigation. He has made that abundantly clear. Even though President Trump has not yet fired Sessions, Mueller, or Rosenstein, his relentless attacks on them are unquestionably an effort to force them to alter their behavior and may already have.

The many federal criminal laws dealing with obstruction of justice share three things, or "elements of the crime." First, they bar influencing, obstructing, or impeding the administration of justice—or even attempting to do so. Second, they require that the interference have a specific object, be it a proceeding or an official. And finally, they require corrupt intent. A wide array of other statutes criminalize specific obstructive behaviors, such as witness tampering, witness retaliation, and covering up, destroying, altering, or falsifying records in an investigation. An impeachment need not prove any violation of these specific statutes; as we have noted previously, impeachment does not require that the president commit a crime. Still, an impeachment for a cover-up or for impeding the administration of justice might want to take notice of the law on obstruction of justice.

THE CASE FOR IMPEACHMENT

The first article of impeachment against Nixon focused on his cover-up of the Watergate burglary by impeding investigations into it. That article did not claim that Nixon violated the federal obstruction of justice or any other criminal statute—even though the cover-up *resembled* the crime of obstruction (and probably was obstruction). As discussed previously, impeachment does not require the commission of a crime, and so the responsibility for dealing with President Trump's possible criminal liability lies with Robert S. Mueller and others, not the House Judiciary Committee.

Nonetheless, it is worth noting that the Watergate grand jury named President Richard Nixon as an unindicted co-conspirator in connection with the prosecution of a number of his top aides, including H. R. Haldeman, his chief of staff; John Ehrlichman, another top White House aide; and John Mitchell, the former attorney general, for obstruction of justice, conspiracy, and perjury. Nixon was the first president to be so named. These defendants were convicted and served prison sentences—in fact, forty-nine people were convicted of crimes related to Watergate, a testament to the breadth of misconduct that occurs when a president enlists his campaign aides, his staff, and his cabinet in a cover-up and other abuses of presidential power.

"Richard M. Nixon," reads the summary of each of his three articles of impeachment, "has acted in a manner contrary to his trust as president and subversive of constitutional government." What follows reads: "to the great prejudice of the cause of law and justice and to the manifest injury of the people of the United States."

While the full scope of President Trump's efforts to impede the investigations into Russian interference in the 2016 presidential election is as yet undetermined, the standard for commencing an impeachment inquiry has been more than met. From the firing of Comey, to the attacks on the investigation, to the release of false exonerating reports and information, to the apparent offers of pardons to keep potential witnesses from talking, Trump's behavior appears to replicate conduct for which a vote to impeach Nixon was taken by the House Judiciary Committee. Significantly, we are not talking in this chapter about isolated incidents, but a far-reaching and continuing groundswell of assaults on the rule of law. Presidents cannot stop an investigation into possible misconduct—they can't pick their investigator or their prosecutor. That was the principle established in the Nixon impeachment, and it is a precedent we need to follow.

We are in an intensely polarized moment in our nation's history, but what we must clearly attend to is that we have a chief executive who is apparently trying to destroy a core democratic value; whose relentless assault on the integrity, independence, and professionalism of our prosecutorial institutions has no modern parallel, and who reduces the might of federal law enforcement to something he can use or manipulate for personal purposes and has the temerity to admit it. In late 2017, he asserted: "I have absolute right to do what I want to do with the Justice Department." He does not; nor do we have to wait until he has succeeded in so doing before we begin an impeachment inquiry.

5

Bribery and Emoluments

President Donald Trump is a rich man who wants to get richer. He is a businessman who is always looking for more business. He is a self-described dealmaker who always wants to make a new deal.

Yet we know very little about his businesses. He was the first president in forty years *not* to release his tax returns. We do know that he runs a business enterprise that uses more than five hundred independent legal entities, or limited liability companies, to receive and spend money on his behalf. His enterprise does business throughout the United States—in New York, Miami, Chicago, California, Hawaii, New Jersey, Virginia, and elsewhere. He has international business operations in more than twenty foreign countries, many of their dealings hidden by the use of corporate camouflages. The voting American public can see few details of the foreign assets he owns—where they are, or what he earns overseas. And it cannot know what foreign bank accounts he might control.

President Trump occupies the most famous office in the world and has an almost unfathomable amount of power: military, financial, legal, bully pulpit. His comments can (and have) crashed corporate stock prices. He can (and did) implement sanctions that would threaten the existence of a company, or he can reverse those sanctions and spare it. He can (and did) approve or deny arms sales abroad. He can launch missiles at foreign countries (and has) without anyone's approval. Companies, individuals, and nations thus have strong incentives to try to influence the president of the United States.

The combination of so much governmental power in the hands of one person with such an extensive, secretive, profit-driven group of companies is a recipe for influence peddling or far worse. Rather than scrupulously or faithfully observing the Constitution, President Trump has rolled out what appears to be a red carpet for those who believe money talks, including foreign governments.

This is something our Constitution's framers feared and tried to prevent. They gave us prohibitions and the powerful remedy of impeachment if nothing else worked.

BRIBERY

Bribery strikes at the heart of democracy and seriously endangers the country. It is one of the constitutionally specified grounds for impeachment for good reason, because a president who is swayed by bribes is no longer acting in the best interests of the country and its people. It was no theoretical concern when the Constitution was being written: the framers knew that King Charles II had secretly been bribed by Louis XIV to ally with France in a war against Holland; Louis XIV also bribed Charles's successor, James II.

Nor is it a theoretical concern today. In 2018 alone, the former New York State assembly speaker and New York senate majority leader were convicted of bribery. One, a Democrat, took nearly $4 million to help researchers at a major university and real estate developers. The other, a Republican, took more than $300,000 to get his son a no-show job from businesses that were dependent on his goodwill and threatened by his official power.

There are a number of publicly reported instances involving President Trump that suggest the possibility of bribery and that could support impeachment. More, non-public information may be in the hands of special counsel Robert Mueller, other branches of the Department of Justice, or our intelligence agencies. All the publicly available instances would require further investigation, which could be undertaken as part of an impeachment inquiry conducted by the House Judiciary Committee or by another committee of the House or Senate. (Non-public information might be turned over to an impeachment inquiry, which happened in Watergate.) As with high crimes and misdemeanors, impeachment for bribery need not be based on a conviction under a specific criminal statute. We do not have to wait for the president to be convicted of bribery before he can be impeached, a seemingly impossible pre-condition for impeachment since the policy of the Department of Justice appears to be that a president cannot be indicted while in office.

President Trump understands and revels in the quid pro quo more than most. "As a businessman and a very substantial donor to very important people, when you give, they do whatever the hell you want them to do," then-candidate Trump told the *Wall Street Journal* in July 2015. "As a businessman, I need that." He made the same point on camera during a debate among the Republican primary candidates. "Before this, before two months ago, I was a businessman. I give to everybody. When they call, I give. And you know what? When I need something from them, two years later, three years later, I call them. They are there for me," he bragged.

Bribery within the meaning of the Constitution's impeachment clause is not implausible when it comes to Trump. He has refused to separate himself from his numerous and far-flung business interests such as hotels and golf courses and is still able, while president, to earn and/or receive money from those businesses. Bribes may easily be disguised in the business context—for example, by overpayments for property, goods, or services. Three recent transactions involving President Trump raise the specter of bribery and should be fully investigated.

Chinese Trademarks

For ten years, Trump and his organization sought Chinese government approval for the registration of numerous trademarks, without success. But on November 13, 2016, five days after his election as president, preliminary approval was granted on a Trump trademark for construction services. On December 2, President-elect Trump took a congratulatory phone call from the president of Taiwan, though no American president had done so since 1979. Nine days later, President-elect Trump stated that the United States might change the One China policy if trade concessions were not forthcoming from China. The Chinese government lodged a formal complaint with the United States.

On February 9, 2017, just before China was to decide on final approval of the trademarks, President Trump suddenly reversed himself. He spoke with China's president and announced he was for the One China policy. Six days later, China's trademark office gave final approval for the construction trademark. On February 27, the day President Trump held his first meeting with a representative of China's government, China announced pending approval of additional trademarks, authorizing the balance on March 6, for a total of thirty-eight trademarks.

Was this bribery on China's part? Was China trying to prevent a possible change in US policy toward Taiwan by approving valuable trademarks for President Trump's business in China? (If Trump were trying to force China to approve the trademarks, then he could have been engaging in extortion, a serious abuse of power and a possible high crime and misde-meanor.) On the other hand, the trademarks could have been an emolu-ment from China—a thing of potential value to demonstrate concretely to President Trump how much it could help his personal business interests (and those of his family) if he would just "play ball" on matters important to China.

President Trump's flip-flopping on Chinese tariffs should be viewed through this lens. Are his decisions affected, delayed, modulated, or influ-enced by various financial enticements China has offered? Are his decisions shaped by its failure to promise or make good on these enticements? The mere suggestion of such concerns erodes confidence in the integrity of our government's and the president's decision-making process.

China/Indonesia Connection

In the spring of 2018, ZTE, a Chinese electronics and telecommunications company, was penalized by the Trump administration's Commerce Depart-ment for defying US sanctions against North Korea and Iran and rewarding company officials for doing so. In addition, the Pentagon announced it was stopping sales of ZTE phones on military bases for national security reasons. ZTE, in response, announced it was going out of business. Then something unusual happened. China announced it was going to invest "bigly" in an Indonesian theme park with which the Trump organization had a licensing deal. Specifically, the Chinese government was going to invest $500 million. Three days later, President Trump, in a surprise announcement, said he wanted to lift the sanctions against ZTE.

At best, President Trump may have violated the emoluments clause of the Constitution by accepting the Chinese government investment in his Indonesian project. At worst, this may be bribery by the Chinese government of President Trump to lift sanctions on ZTE.

Kushner/Qatar

According to online news publication *The Intercept*, the father of Jared Kushner, President Trump's son-in-law, urged the Qatari finance minister in April 2017 to provide financing for 666 Fifth Avenue in New York City, a building Kushner had bought at an excessive price and that was in serious financial trouble. Qatar refused.

In June, a coalition of Middle Eastern countries announced a blockade against Qatar. President Trump sided with the coalition—against the position of his own State Department and despite the fact that the largest US military facility in the Middle East is located there—and called Qatar a "funder of terrorism at a very high level." Roughly a year later, on April 10, 2018, President Trump did an about-face, calling Qatar's leader a "great friend"; then, about a month later, Kushner's father announced a financing deal for 666 Fifth Avenue with a major partner of the Qatari government. Was this blackmail by President Trump—again, in itself a serious abuse of power and a likely impeachable offense? Was this the payment of a bribe by Qatar to President Trump's son-in-law, also an impeachable offense? Was it an emolument to both Kushner and President Trump? Likewise, a possibly impeachable offense.

The Meaning of Bribery and the Impeachment Clause

Criminal bribery law is extensive and complex. In the last decade, federal bribery statutes have been narrowly construed by the courts, and a recent Supreme Court decision involving a former Virginia governor has made it much more difficult for criminal prosecutions to succeed. Today, prosecutors need to prove that a politician undertook discrete, identifiable official actions for a bribe. In short, buying "access and ingratiation" is now legal under our federal criminal law. Under the law, however, the bribed-for action need not be taken. For example, agreeing to vote a certain way in exchange for money is criminal even if the vote never takes place.

But that is criminal law, concerning imprisonment of elected officials for extreme, reprehensible behavior. Impeachment law is different. It is about protecting our nation and our Constitution from grievous injury at the hands of a corrupt officeholder. No individuals go to prison as a result of impeachment, but they do get removed from office.

Bribery is not defined in the Constitution. The first two federal bribery laws were passed in 1789 and 1790 and dealt only with bribing judges and customs officials. The first law barring bribery of federal legislators was not passed until 1853. A generally applicable anti-bribery federal statute was not passed until the twentieth century.

Under the 1790 law, the elements of bribery are clear: giving something of value in exchange for an official act is a bribe. Bribery laws were, however, largely honored in the breach throughout the nineteenth century. The first notable high-level prosecution for bribery came in the 1920s, when the secretary of the interior, Albert Bacon Fall, was convicted in the Teapot Dome scandal.

The current principal federal bribery statute, 18 U.S.C. § 201(b), does not differ significantly from the earlier ones. It provides for the imprisonment of a public official who "directly or indirectly, corruptly demands, seeks, receives, accepts, or agrees to receive or accept anything of value personally or for any other person or entity, in return for . . . being influenced in the performance of any official act . . ."

Congress may not be strictly bound in an impeachment proceeding by the elements of the current federal bribery statutes or the recent Supreme Court decisions interpreting them. But impeachment for taking bribes should nonetheless encompass the knowing receipt by a president of money or something of value designed to affect the president's official behavior—whether the president's behavior is affected or not. This is the gist of bribery. The examples of ZTE, Qatar, and Chinese trademarks discussed previously would need to be carefully investigated and evaluated to see if they fit this definition.

EMOLUMENTS

As with *bribery*, the framers of the Constitution provide no definition of *emoluments*, which are first cousins of bribery. They so strongly feared that emoluments would carve a path to corruption that they wrote two provisions to guard against it: one to bar the taking of emoluments from foreign governments and another to bar their receipt from states and the United States government. An antique curiosity of a word, its elusiveness had a federal judge himself thumbing through dictionaries in the case of *The District of Columbia and the State of Maryland v. Donald Trump*, a suit claiming "unprecedented constitutional violations" by Donald Trump arising from his receipt of income from foreign and state government at the Trump International Hotel in Washington. (Three of his children own 22.5 percent of the hotel combined. He owns the rest.) Evaluating the historical record, the court found that "an 'emolument' was commonly understood by the founding generation to encompass 'profit,' 'gain,' or 'advantage.'"

"Though the Court agrees that mere counting of dictionaries may not be dispositive," the decision stated, "it nonetheless remains highly remarkable that [here Georgetown University Law School professor and associate dean John

Mikhail was quoted] 'every English dictionary definition of "emolument" from 1604 to 1806 relies on one or more of the elements of th[is] broad definition.'"

It is worth considering why the two emoluments clauses were incorporated into the Constitution. It seems quite simple: the Founders regarded emoluments as bribes in the making. At the time the Constitution was drafted, the framers were "deeply concerned that foreign interests would try to use their wealth to tempt public servants and sway the foreign policy decisions of the new government," according to Fordham law professor Zephyr Teachout. They saw the same problem with payments from domestic governments.

The clauses were critical inoculations against outright bribery or even more subtle but just as worrying influence peddling. Bribery is often hard to prove. The Founders wanted government officials to steer well clear of any hint of bribes, especially from foreign governments. The best way to do that is straightforward: do not take their money.

The foreign emoluments clause was advocated by South Carolina's Charles Pinckney, citing "the necessity of preserving foreign Ministers & other officers of the US independent of external influence." Later, while Virginia was debating ratification of the Constitution, future attorney general Edmund Randolph opined that "[t]his restriction was provided to prevent corruption."

During the same Virginia debates, George Mason worried that it would be "difficult to know whether [the executive] receives emoluments from foreign powers or not," and that "the great powers of Europe" would "be interested in having a friend in the President of the United States." In doing so, he anticipated the exact problem posed by President Trump's far-flung business interests and his refusal to separate himself from them. As a 1987 Department of Justice study of the history of the foreign emolument clause and compliance with it concluded: "[c]onsistent with its expansive language and underlying purpose, the [foreign emolument] provision has been interpreted as being 'particularly directed against every kind of influence by foreign *governments* upon offices of the United States, based upon our historic policies as a nation.'" As we'll see below, the pattern of foreign government payments and benefits to President Trump since his inauguration exemplifies "every kind of influence that was condemned."

The foreign emoluments clause provides that

[n]o title of Nobility shall be granted by the United States: And no person holding any Office of Profit of Trust under them, shall,

without the Consent of the Congress, accept of any present, Emolument, Office, or Title, of any kind whatever, from any King, Prince, or foreign state. (Article I, Section 9, Clause 8)

While under the Constitution emoluments from a foreign government are prohibited unless approved by Congress, emoluments from the United States or from any state (Article II, Section 1, Clause 7) are banned entirely:

> The President shall, at stated Times, receive for his Services, a Compensation, which shall neither be encreased nor diminished during the Period for which he shall have been elected, and he shall not receive within that Period any other Emolument from the United States, or any of them.

The impeachment proceedings against Richard Nixon, a very useful blueprint for inquiry into President Trump's possible impeachment, are of less help with respect to emoluments. During that inquiry, the House Judiciary Committee obtained information about emoluments received by President Richard Nixon. The evidence uncovered by another House committee showed improvements made to Nixon's personal properties in Key Biscayne, Florida, and San Clemente, California, at the federal government's expense. The IRS estimated that the income Nixon received from these improvements during the years 1969–72 amounted to $67,000. The staff of the Joint Committee on Internal Revenue Taxation estimated the total at $92,000. (The improvements included reconstruction of a shuffleboard court, landscaping items, and a heating system, among other things.) An article of impeachment was proposed against President Nixon on the grounds that these "non-protective government expenditures" were for his "personal enrichment." It was defeated, 16–12.

Significantly, nobody on the Judiciary Committee questioned whether a president *could* be impeached for violating the emoluments clause. Rather, the majority voted against the article because there was "no direct evidence" that President Nixon was aware that payments had been made from public, not private, funds (the requests had been made by the Secret Service), and because it "did not rise to the level of an impeachable offense," probably because the dollar amounts were relatively insubstantial. The offense was probably seen as less egregious than those described in the other articles of impeachment voted by the committee.

The Nixon example pales in comparison to the emolument concerns raised about President Trump, whose retention of a financial interest in his far-flung businesses at a minimum creates the appearance that foreign agents or government are currying favor with him or, as in the case of the Chinese trademark approvals, awarding valuable items that might be payoffs. Keeping the president free of this kind of foreign influence—and the appearance of it—was a major worry of the Constitution's framers. President Trump's refusal to attend to this concern—in fact, his total disdain for it—is what makes his treatment of emoluments a great and dangerous offense. The porous line between his personal and governmental business, particularly in the area of foreign affairs, poses an imminent danger to America, and his steadfast refusal to rectify the problem may constitute a high crime and misdemeanor.

President Trump has made no serious attempt to comply with the Constitution's emoluments clauses. He has hidden and obfuscated the nature of his business holdings and payments to them. He continues to draw income from his businesses. Although he has been offered multiple ways to remedy these violations and urged repeatedly to do so, he has chosen not to. Indeed, there is evidence that suggests President Trump has encouraged and sought emoluments. Perhaps above all, he has accepted emoluments without asking for congressional approval, flagrantly violating the Constitution.

Foreign Emoluments

President Trump has numerous foreign financial entanglements. Many of them involve foreign governments. Not surprisingly, the Trump International Hotel in Washington, DC, the subject of the State of Maryland lawsuit previously mentioned, is the epicenter of many an apparent violation of the foreign emoluments clause.

Foreign governments appear to believe that giving President Trump money through this hotel is a surefire way to curry favor and affect his judgment. Even before the inauguration, foreign government officials were looking to spend money at the president-elect's hotel. "'Why wouldn't I stay at his hotel blocks from the White House, so I can tell the new president, 'I love your new hotel!' Isn't it rude to come to his city and say, 'I am staying at your competitor?'" an Asian diplomat told the *Washington Post* shortly after the election. The newspaper went on to report: "In interviews with a dozen diplomats, many of whom declined to be named because they were not authorized to speak about anything related to the next US president, some said spending money at Trump's hotel is an easy, friendly gesture to the new president."

"Friendly gesture" is a nice way of saying "buy influence." At least one diplomat interviewed by the *Washington Post* laid out the thinking clearly: "'The temptation and the inclination will certainly be there,' said Arturo Sarukhan, a former Mexican ambassador to the United States. 'Some might think it's the right way to engage, to be able to tell the next president, 'Oh, I stayed at your hotel.' If I were still in government, I would discourage it, among other reasons because it can be questioned and looked at in a very poor light, as though you are trying to buy influence via a hotel bill.'"

Indeed, the Trump Organization was quick to capitalize on foreign government eagerness. Eleven days after the election, it hosted a reception to promote the hotel to about one hundred foreign diplomats, and a "director of diplomatic sales" was hired to facilitate business with foreign states and their diplomats and agents. One former ambassador later reported hearing that the State Department was pressuring foreign diplomats to stay there.

Foreign dignitaries and diplomats who have stayed at or used the Trump International for various functions or meals include those from:

- Georgia: The ambassador and permanent representative to the United Nations stayed at Trump International (April 2017);
- Kuwait: The country has twice celebrated its National Day at the hotel (February 2017 and February 2018);
- Malaysia: Prime Minister Najib Razak and members of his delegation rented conference rooms and appeared to stay overnight (September 2017);
- The Philippines: The embassy hosted its National Day at the hotel (June 2018);
- Romania: President Klaus Iohannis and his wife, Carmen Iohannis, enjoyed breakfast in the hotel lobby (June 2017);
- Saudi Arabia: Consultants and hired protesters spent $268,000 at the hotel for several months of lobbying against US antiterrorism legislation, according to public filings—including, notably, shortly after the early June 2017 blockade against Qatar, of which President Trump tweeted his implicit approval; and

- Turkey: The US-Turkey Business Council, which is controlled by the Turkish government, held its annual conference at the hotel (May 2017).

There are other examples: Greek officials in town to celebrate their nation's Independence Day at the White House stayed at the hotel (March 2018); an official from the Dominican Republic was seen dining at the hotel (March 2018); Turkey's foreign minister appears to have stayed at the hotel during the inauguration (January 2017). Ambassadors from Russia, the United Arab Emirates, and Turkey have also been spotted at the Trump International.

This type of foreign government activity is precisely what the framers sought to forestall by including the foreign emoluments clause. To be sure, some diplomats might just like the hotel above all others in Washington, DC. Many might regard staying at or having dinner there as merely a "friendly gesture." Others certainly will regard it as a way to buy influence or access outright.

The Trump International Hotel has succeeded in charging more for its rooms since the inauguration. According to the *Washington Post*, in 2017 "guests have paid an average of $652.98 a night to stay there, beating the company's expectations by 57 percent. . . . That probably makes it the most expensive hotel in the city." While the average room rate for non-Trump hotels in the United States increased 2.3 percent in 2017, and rates across all the hotels bearing his name have dropped sharply—25 percent on average—the DC Trump International is an exception, its unique success undoubtedly buoyed by its place as an ideal vehicle for providing benefits to the president.

Likely in response to public concern, President Trump has claimed that he can avoid violating the foreign emoluments clause by donating the profits made from foreign government guests. In March 2018, the Trump Organization said it would pay $151,000 to the US Treasury, the amount it claimed was the profit it earned from foreign government use of his Washington hotel. But there was no backup information to verify the calculations—and the Trump Organization had stated previously that it would only estimate the amounts, in any case. Nothing in the Constitution appears to permit turning over only profits to the Treasury—and estimated ones at that. Moreover, any use of a hotel room in the Trump International is a likely benefit, meaning the entire price is an emolument, since an empty room is a loss.

The Trump International is not the only site of the president's apparent receipt of foreign emoluments. He receives $1.9 million in annual rental revenue at Trump Tower in New York City from the Industrial & Commercial Bank of China, whose majority owner is the Chinese government. The bank's offices are six floors below the president's own Trump Tower space, and it is the largest commercial tenant in the building. In 2019, its lease will be over, meaning that, according to a February 2018 *Forbes* article, "Eric Trump and Donald Trump Jr. could well be negotiating right now over how many millions the Chinese government will pay the sitting president."

In January 2018, the government of Qatar paid $6.5 million for an apartment in the Trump World Tower, bringing its total to four units with a cumulative cost of $16.5 million. The Trump Organization receives monthly fees from the tenants in the building. Other governments own units there or regularly use its facilities. The Afghan, Indian, Qatari, and Saudi Arabian governments pay more than $225,000 a year in building-related charges to the Trump Organization.

In March 2018, Saudi Crown Prince Mohammed bin Salman booked a five-day stay at the Trump International Hotel in New York City. Prior to his stay, the hotel had experienced a two-year revenue decrease; the Saudi prince's stay was enough to reverse the trend, driving revenue up 13 percent for the first quarter of the year, according to a report from the hotel's general manager obtained by the *Washington Post*. In August 2018, the New York attorney general's office confirmed that it was investigating whether the stay was an emolument and whether to sue President Trump as a result.

Trump Indonesia: The Trump Organization is developing two hotel and golf course properties in Bali and Lido. According to one analyst, those resorts are the beneficiaries of six potential emoluments: 1) more than 1,500 acres of public land have been granted to the developments; 2) two toll roads are being constructed for them by a state-owned company (the land that the access road runs over is farmland that was sold as a result of government pressure); 3) the government granted broad, normally hard-to-obtain permits to build inside a national park; 4) legal requirements for an environmental impact assessment and building code restrictions for construction on oceanfront cliffs were waived; 5) the land-use zoning was altered from agriculture or watershed to tourism; 6) the government is apparently refusing to enforce many environmental regulations. All told, President Trump has reported $2–$10 million in revenue from the two projects, which are not yet even completed.

In addition, the Trump hotels and golf courses now stand to benefit from a newly announced theme park, announced in May 2018 and due to be built by a Chinese government–owned construction company, with $500 million of its funding coming from the Chinese government.

Trump Towers Istanbul: The two towers were constructed in the last decade. President Trump licensed his name to the developer, Dogan Holdings, and continues to receive revenue from it, up to $1 million last year. A $2.5 billion fine for unpaid taxes, however, has been imposed on Dogan Holdings by the Turkish government. If aggressively pursued, the fine could dramatically affect President Trump's revenue from the project. According to a *Newsweek* report, Turkey's President Recep Tayyip Erdogan "told associates he believes he must keep pressure on Trump's business partner [in Turkey] to essentially blackmail the president."

Trump Tower Manila: The $150 million, 57-story residential tower is nearing completion, and sales are under way. President Trump's business partner in the development is effectively a government official: in late 2016, Philippine president Rodrigo Duterte appointed Jose E. B. Antonio, special envoy to Washington for trade.

Trump Ocean Club International Hotel & Tower, Panama City: In March 2018, the Trump Organization management team in Panama City was ejected from the property. The company's lawyers then wrote a letter to the president of Panama warning that the matter "has repercussions for the Panamanian state, which is your responsibility." The Trump Organization deal in Panama ended in the summer of 2018. Before the collapse of that deal, the Trump Organization had benefited from government favors and actions, including use of the hotel for government functions and government repair of private drainage and sewage systems around the building after a private contractor declared bankruptcy.

These examples may be the tip of the iceberg. President Trump's companies do business around the world, sometimes with other companies controlled by foreign governments. Often the deals and interactions are shrouded in secrecy. For example, though the Trump Organization sold more than $35 million in real estate in the United States in 2017, the identities of some purchasers are cloaked by the use of limited liability companies. Two years prior to Trump's nomination, according to a *USA Today* investigation, 4 percent of Trump property purchasers used legal tools to obscure their identity. In 2017, 70 percent did.

Domestic Emoluments

President Trump has not said whether or how he will deal with emoluments from state officials or from agencies of the United States, such as the State Department. Unlike foreign emoluments, they cannot be remedied by congressional approval or anything else. They are entirely prohibited, as noted above.

Payments resulting from at least five incidents may amount to domestic emoluments:

- At least one governor of a state has stayed at the Trump DC hotel on official business.
- Tax concessions were given to the Trump Organization by the District of Columbia.
- The State Department appears to have scheduled events for visiting groups that it brings to the United States at the Trump International Hotel in Washington, DC. Amounts accruing to President Trump in this manner are not known, but a Freedom of Information Act request has been lodged with the State Department.
- The federal General Services Administration (GSA) determined that the Trump Organization's lease of the Old Post Office, now the Trump International Hotel, is valid despite a provision stipulating that "no official of the government of the United States shall be admitted to any share or part of this lease." The GSA decided—after President Trump took office and his appointee took over the agency—that the provision was no bar because a new provision in the hotel's operating agreement prohibited any distributions to him while he was in office, and because he removed himself from management of any of the Trump companies involved in the lease. Does this flimsy reasoning reflect an arm's-length, objective analysis—when the GSA was headed by President Trump's own appointee? Or, rather, is it an emolument—because the president will still receive his share of the revenues, although receipt is postponed? The Constitution does not allow emoluments that are deferred; that would be a loophole that would swallow the rule.
- In Mississippi, a hotel development managed by the Trump Organization asked for and received a $6 million tax break from the state.

President Trump Maintains an Active Interest in His Business Holdings

President Trump is president and business owner at the same time. He has not given up or altered ownership of his businesses since his inauguration and is still involved in their operation. Though the full extent of his involvement is not clear, he remains engaged.

Before his inauguration, President Trump made it clear that he did not take the potential emoluments and conflicts of interest raised by his business activities seriously. "I could actually run my business and run government at the same time. I don't like the way that looks," he said. "But I would be able to do that if I wanted to." He told the *New York Times*: "In theory I could run my business perfectly and then run the country perfectly."

He established a trust to hold his business assets and said he would turn over the "leadership and management" of his companies to his two sons. The trust instrument has not been publicly released, but his lawyers have confirmed that he can withdraw money from it at any time and can dispose of assets in it as he chooses. He also can revoke the trust whenever he wants.

He promised the American public that his sons would not discuss business with him. "What I'm going to be doing is my two sons, who are right here, Don and Eric, are going to be running the company," President-elect Trump said at a January 2017 news conference. "They are going to be running it in a very professional manner. They're not going to discuss it with me."

Yet, a few months later, Eric indicated that he provides his father regular updates. He spoke to *Forbes* magazine, which reported that "he will continue to update his father on the business while he is president. 'Yeah [Eric said], on the bottom line, profitability reports and stuff like that, but you know, that's about it.' How often will those reports be, every quarter? 'Depending, yeah, depending.' Could be more, could be less? 'Yeah, probably quarterly.' One thing is clear: 'My father and I are very close,' Eric Trump says. 'I talk to him a lot. We're pretty inseparable.'"

Eric Trump is not the only person to report interactions with President Trump about his business. In late 2017, the director of revenue management for the Trump International Hotel in Washington wrote, in an email obtained by the *Washington Post*:

> The company is interesting to work for being under the Trump umbrella. DJT is supposed to be out of the business and passed on to

his sons, but he's definitely still involved . . . so it's interesting and unique in that way. I had a brief meeting with him a few weeks ago, and he was asking about banquet revenues and demographics. And, he asked if his presidency hurt the businesses. So, he seems self aware about things, at least more than he lets on. I am far left leaning politically, so working here has been somewhat of a challenge for me. But, it's all business.

President Trump continues to boost his businesses. For example, in his first year in office, he or his staff promoted one of his properties or brands fifty-four times. He publicized his New Jersey golf club while giving a speech to the South Korean parliament. He touted a winery he owns in Virginia while discussing the violence that left one person dead at the August 2017 neo-Nazi rally in nearby Charlottesville. He also visits his properties regularly. As of mid-July 2018, he had spent 170 days at his various properties on visits ranging far and wide: a few hours at a Hawaii property while en route to Asia; three days at his Scottish golf course while waiting to meet with Russian president Vladimir Putin; fourteen times at the Trump International Hotel, in Washington; and days at golf courses and hotels up and down the East Coast. Use of his official powers to promote his private business interests, if sufficiently systematic and widespread, could amount to an abuse of power.

More recently, President Trump has been personally involved in decisions regarding federal property a block from the Trump International Hotel. For almost a decade, the GSA, which manages federal property, had planned to move FBI headquarters. One thought was to raze the building, an option that would cause considerable disruption. The site would subsequently become available for development.

In the summer of 2017, however, the relocation plan was canceled; in February 2018, it was announced that FBI headquarters would remain at the site, though the building would still be taken down. According to news website Axios, "[f]or months [in 2018], in meetings with White House officials and the Senate, [a House Appropriations subcommittee] intended to discuss big-picture spending priorities, [but] the president rants about the graceless" FBI building. In late August, the GSA's inspector general issued a report indicating that a GSA official had delivered incomplete and possibly misleading testimony to Congress about the involvement of the president and the White House in the project but had also refused to answer any questions from the internal investigators about those meetings. If the federal government's decision regarding the FBI building were intended to help President Trump's DC Hotel, that could violate the emoluments clause. It might also be an abuse of power for the president to interfere with federal building plans in order to benefit his personal business interests.

The Emoluments Lawsuits Against President Trump

President Trump's lawyers have spent considerable time in court and in legal briefs arguing that commercial transactions with foreign governments are not emoluments. The arguments not only defy common sense, but make light of the acute understanding of human nature that our Founders had: commercial transactions build ties of loyalty and gratitude. Our president should have only one loyalty: to the American people. He should not be flattered or influenced by foreign governments that spend money on him, whether at his hotels or by giving him gold medals. Centuries of presidential and official practice, the meaning of the emoluments clauses, and American history demonstrate that the president is violating the Constitution.

Three days after President Trump was sworn into office, he was sued for violating the emoluments clauses. Since then, two additional major lawsuits have been brought. Each has faced a different fate in court.

Citizens for Responsibility and Ethics in Washington v. Donald Trump was filed on January 23, 2017, in New York. Claiming violation of both emoluments clauses, the plaintiffs—collectively referred to by the acronym CREW— spoke both to the clauses' history and to their current relevance:

> As the Framers were aware, private financial interests can subtly sway even the most virtuous leaders, and entanglements between American officials and foreign powers could pose a creeping, insidious threat to the Republic. The Foreign Emoluments Clause was forged of the Framers' hard-won wisdom. It is no relic of a bygone era, but rather an expression of insight into the nature of the human condition and the preconditions of self-governance.

CREW was joined in succeeding months by a number of plaintiffs claiming that their businesses face unfair competition from Trump properties, and amicus briefs were filed by legal historians, members of Congress, and national security officials. On December 21, 2017, a New York federal district court dismissed the lawsuit, stating that the plaintiffs did not have standing—that is, were not able to demonstrate a clear injury to themselves as a result of the defendant's actions. The concept of standing, in effect, prohibits theoretical disputes between parties. CREW is appealing the decision.

The District of Columbia and the State of Maryland v. Donald Trump was filed on June 12, 2017, in Maryland. It was brought by the attorneys general of both states. They alleged:

> President Trump's continued ownership interest in a global business empire, which renders him deeply enmeshed with a legion of foreign and domestic government actors, violates the Constitution and calls into question the rule of law and the integrity of the country's political system. . . . [I]rrespective of whether such benefits affect the President's decision-making or shift his foreign or domestic policy, uncertainty about whether the President is acting in the best interests of the American people, or rather for his own ends or personal enrichment, inflicts lasting harm on our democracy.

As discussed elsewhere in this chapter, the district court allowed the lawsuit to proceed, holding that the plaintiffs had standing and that they had made a legal case that the payments by foreign governments at the Trump hotel in DC are emoluments.

Blumenthal v. Donald Trump was filed on June 15, 2017, in Washington, DC. It was brought by Senator Richard Blumenthal of Connecticut and 194 other senators and representatives. They alleged:

> Because the Foreign Emoluments Clause requires the President to obtain "the Consent of the Congress" before accepting otherwise prohibited "Emolument[s]," Plaintiffs, as members of Congress, must have the opportunity to cast a binding vote that gives or withholds their "Consent" before the President accepts any such "Emolument. . . ."
>
> Because Defendant has failed to come to Congress and seek its consent for at least some foreign emoluments that have been the subject of public reporting, it is impossible to know whether

Defendant has also accepted, or plans to accept, other foreign uments that have not yet been made public. By accepting the benefits from foreign states without first seeking or obtaining congressional approval, Defendant has thwarted the transparency that the "Consent of the Congress" provision was designed to provide.

The president filed a motion to dismiss the suit, which the district court rejected, deciding that the senator and his colleagues had the standing to bring it.

In each of these cases, the Department of Justice has represented President Trump. He has also hired private attorneys to represent him. The Justice Department lawyers are involved in the matter for one simple reason: they are obliged to defend presidents against lawsuits when they are sued in their official capacity. They are taking the president's side against Congress because it is their job to do so.

The lawsuit that has proceeded furthest is *The District of Columbia and the State of Maryland v. Donald Trump*. Consequently, the filings by President Trump's Department of Justice lawyers are the best explanation we have of why he thinks he is not violating the emoluments clauses.

According to his filings, "the Emoluments Clauses only prohibit the receipt of compensation for services rendered by an official in an official capacity or in an employment (or equivalent) relationship with a foreign government, and the receipt of honors and gifts by an officeholder from a foreign government."

In short, President Trump believes he would violate the emoluments clauses only if he accepted money from a foreign government in a direct exchange for an official act as president (in other words, a bribe)—or if he were employed by a foreign government, a point that is not relevant here. By that standard, a foreign government could chose to rent out the Trump International Hotel ballroom for $1 million, take out an ad in the *Washington Post* advertising the event, and pay President Trump to make a personal speech there—and yet it would not trigger the foreign emoluments clause. Why? Because the clause "does not reach benefits arising from commercial transactions engaged in by businesses in which the President has a financial interest," the president's legal brief asserted.

President Trump's flawed argument can be boiled down to two simple points.

First, only outright bribery—the most egregious and offensive corruption—is prohibited by the clauses. His brief notes, "[f]or example, a federal official would receive an emolument if he or she was paid by a foreign government to take certain official actions." The president claimed that nothing more can be construed as an emolument.

This argument, which flies in the face of the historical record and makes a mockery of a key provision in the Constitution, simply cannot be taken seriously. As the court noted in rejecting it, the president's position "is tantamount to defining the transaction [that is, an emolument] as nothing less than one of federal bribery." But think of it. The foreign emoluments clause allows Congress to approve a foreign emolument or not approve it. So, if an emolument is basically a bribe, the president wants us to believe that the Constitution allows a federal official, in effect, to be bribed as long as Congress okays it. That is patently absurd.

The president's second argument is that his commercial enterprises are complicated—too complicated for him to try to comply with the Constitution and too complicated for a court to deal with. His brief complains: "Plaintiffs challenge everything from a single diplomat's payment for hospitality services to any trademarks, permits, licenses, and approvals that may be granted by foreign governments in connection with the commercial activities of the President's business organization in numerous countries."

While the brief is right—the plaintiffs do raise concerns about many transactions because all of them are potentially emoluments—this line of reasoning from the president is simply not credible. He is a sophisticated businessman. He presumably has created compliance systems at his numerous properties and businesses dealing with global labor, banking, construction, and environmental regulations, to name a few. He has managed to create a business with more than five hundred separate operating legal entities. He runs complex hotel systems that can itemize every customer transaction from the moment of reservation to the moment that peanuts are taken out of a minibar. Does he really expect us to believe that he can't build a system that will comply with the Constitution?

The district court in Maryland rejected the president's position. It held "that the term 'emolument' in both Clauses extends to *any profit, gain, or advantage* [emphasis mine] of more than *de minimis* value, received by him, directly or indirectly, from foreign, the federal, or domestic governments. This includes profits from private transactions, even those involving services given at fair market value."

Recently, another federal official, besides President Trump, failed to take the foreign emoluments clause seriously. For more than a decade, Guam's delegate to the House of Representatives, Madeleine Z. Bordallo, has been renting a home in Guam to the Japanese consul. In June 2017, the Office of Congressional Ethics voted to refer her for investigation for violating House ethics rules. (Bordallo is a nonvoting member of the House of Representatives). While admittedly applying to members of Congress and not a president, the House Ethics Manual addresses emoluments. Defining an emolument as any "profit, gain, or compensation for services rendered," the manual stipulates: "Members and employees may not therefore receive any payment for services rendered to official foreign interests, such as ambassadors, embassies, or agencies of a foreign government."

In the almost 230 years since the Constitution was adopted, numerous presidents, members of Congress, and others holding high federal office all have made meticulous efforts to check whether they are complying with the emoluments clauses and have made necessary business arrangements to avoid violating them.

The emoluments clauses are not abstract or obscure provisions, even though they are not widely known by the public at large. Before President Trump, American presidents and high-ranking federal officials took the provisions seriously.

In 1840, when the sultan of Oman sent President Martin Van Buren two Arabian horses, a rug, a sword, pearls, and a shawl, he declined them. The president, the secretary of state, and the consul based in Oman all persistently tried to turn down the valuable goods. They spent almost a year trying to avoid taking an emolument. The president wrote to the sultan that "a fundamental law of the Republic" barred such presents. After it was clear that something had to be done with the items, Van Buren wrote to Congress and asked permission to accept them: "I deem it my duty to lay the proposition before Congress for such disposition as they may think fit to make of it."

A few years later, President John Tyler was given two horses from the sultan of Oman, then called Muscat and Oman. As with his predecessor, he followed the rules laid out by the Constitution and reported the gifts to Congress. Congress directed him to auction off the horses and give the proceeds to the Treasury.

Less than twenty years later, President Abraham Lincoln notified Congress when the king of Siam sent him a sword, two elephant tusks, and some pictures. Congress directed him to consign the items to the Interior Department.

President Benjamin Harrison asked Congress about medals presented to him by Brazil and Spain. Congress authorized him to keep them in 1896.

In 1981, President Ronald Reagan was concerned that accepting his pension from the State of California might violate the domestic emoluments clause. He sought guidance from the Department of Justice and the comptroller general, who heads the Government Accountability Office, an arm of Congress. They both concluded that it was not an emolument, since the pension was a "vested right" rather than a "gratuity which the State is free to withdraw." The distinction was important because there was no risk that the state might use the financial relationship for influence, and there was no possibility that President Reagan would feel any sense of dependency on the state.

In 2009, when President Barack Obama was due to accept the Nobel Peace Prize and its award money, he sought guidance from the Department of Justice, as well. It concluded, as we have seen, that the prize was not an emolument because the money did not come from a foreign government.

THE IMPEACHABILITY OF PRESIDENT TRUMP'S ALLEGED EMOLUMENTS VIOLATIONS

Under normal circumstances, accepting a single small emolument might not warrant impeachment. But President Trump appears to have received multiple emoluments, has made an effort to cover them up, and has even seemed actively to seek and revel in emoluments. He has crafted a patently absurd justification for accepting them that shows contempt for constitutional restrictions on being influenced by business opportunities and profiting from office. Given the frequency and scale of the emoluments, and his refusal to seek the congressional approval for foreign emoluments that is constitutionally mandated before accepting them, his actions should be viewed as a systematic attempt to subvert the Constitution.

President Trump had many options for dealing with the emoluments he receives. He could have divested. He could have sold his businesses. He could have created an accounting and billing system to avoid accepting payments from foreign governments. He could have asked Congress for permission under the foreign emoluments clause, which requires congressional approval before an emolument may be received. By requiring approval, the

Founders sought to ensure transparency and honesty about potential monetary entanglements between officeholders and foreign governments, and to permit a neutral evaluation of the potential impact. And does anyone doubt that a Congress controlled by members of his party would have allowed him to accept appropriate commercial foreign emoluments? Had he chosen simply to ask for permission as laid out in the Constitution, and received it, there would be no question of impeachment.

He is currently the defendant in three lawsuits attempting to hold him to account for violating the clauses, and the General Services Administration inspector general is still investigating whether the agency's decision to allow him to maintain the lease of the Trump International Hotel in Washington was properly made. American taxpayers are footing the bill for at least ten government lawyers and support staff arguing in support of his private business interests.

We do not know whether President Trump is aware of each individual emolument he has received. But he does not need to be for impeachment. He is well aware of the constitutional mandate and has orchestrated a full-scale battle against it, involving lawsuits, feeble proposed workarounds (donating estimated profits to the Treasury), and meaningless solutions (a trust he can revoke at any time).

This behavior:

- reveals a disrespect for a core constitutional provision designed to prevent corruption or its appearance in the presidency;
- has a corrosive effect on public confidence in the integrity of the decisions made by President Trump and his administration; and
- opens American foreign policy up to the scorn of nations, many of which have come to believe that presidential policy decisions can be obtained by offering business deals or other monetary benefits to the president.

For these reasons, President Trump's many and constant apparent violations of the emoluments clauses should be seen as likely high crimes and misdemeanors.

Our Founders certainly would have thought so. During the Constitutional Convention in Philadelphia, Gouverneur Morris—no friend of the impeachment clause—explained why he had changed his mind and come to support it. He feared the president "may be bribed by a greater interest to betray his trust; and no one would say that we ought to expose ourselves to the danger of seeing the first Magistrate in foreign pay, without being able to guard agst. it by displacing him."

During the Virginia ratification debates, George Mason, the framer most responsible for the impeachment clause as it was finally drafted, warned that "the great powers of Europe" might corrupt the president the way Russia had corrupted Poland. "Will not the great powers of Europe, as France and Great Britain, be interested in having a friend in the President of the United States?" Mason asked. "It is not many years ago—since the revolution—that a foreign power offered emoluments to persons holding offices under our government. It will, moreover, be difficult to know whether he receives emoluments from foreign powers or not," he continued.

"There is [a] provision against the danger mentioned by the honorable member, of the president receiving emoluments from foreign powers," future attorney general Edmund Randolph answered. "If discovered, he may be impeached."

We know that the framers intended the remedy of impeachment for violations of the emoluments clauses. Given the evidence of President Trump's systematic and ongoing receipt of emoluments, both domestic and foreign, and the danger it creates for the United States, the case for an inquiry into whether the president should be impeached is clear-cut.

6

Other Possibly Impeachable Acts

The preceding chapters regarding election interference, obstruction of justice, and emoluments represent what I consider the three strongest potential grounds for impeaching President Trump. Three other possibilities for impeachment have been raised:

The president may have committed treason by colluding with Russia to get elected;

The president may have abused the power of his office by approving the separation of several thousand children from their parents after they crossed the US-Mexico border, in violation of their constitutional rights; and

The president may have won his election corruptly by allegedly conspiring to conceal his extramarital affairs from the voters through payments of hush money and other possible violations of campaign finance laws.

I do *not* believe that the evidence of treason/collusion is sufficient for impeachment at this time. I *do* think that the president's decision to separate children from their parents at the border may well be impeachable. And while new facts are constantly emerging about the cover-up of the president's alleged affairs and related possible violations of campaign finance laws, I feel that the standard for impeachment has *not* yet been met for this particular set of offenses.

Collusion or Conspiracy with Russia to Subvert an Election: Treason or High Crime and Misdemeanor?

President Trump and Vladimir Putin in Helsinki

President Trump's extremely troubling responses to Russia's election interference and his campaign's multiple contacts with agents of that country's government are well known and detailed in Chapters 3 and 4. While "treason" was rarely used to describe them, that word cropped up often after President Trump's astonishing statements during a press conference following his two-hour closed-door meeting with Russian president Vladimir Putin in Helsinki on July 16, 2018. This is what he said:

> My people came to me. Dan Coats came to me and some others. They said they think it's Russia. I have President Putin; he just said it's not Russia. I will say this: I don't see any reason why it would be. . . . I have great confidence in my intelligence people, but I will tell you that President Putin was extremely strong and powerful in his denial today.

The statement left many Americans aghast. Three days earlier, a federal grand jury had indicted twelve Russian military intelligence officers for attacking the 2016 presidential election. Five months earlier, a different federal indictment had charged thirteen other Russian individuals and three companies with using social media to foment unrest in an effort to influence the election. And in January 2017, US intelligence agency heads briefed President-elect Trump that the Russian government, at Putin's direction, had interfered in the election to help him and hurt Hillary Clinton. They had reiterated their position in congressional testimony throughout 2017 and well into 2018. Social media companies conducted their own investigations and concurred. Congressional committees, too, had found independently that Russia had assaulted the US election system and manipulated public opinion.

Although President Trump has denied any collusion with Russia's election interference and denigrated Mueller's investigation of it often and forcefully, after publicly (and meekly) siding with Putin in Helsinki, he faced a barrage of charges of treason. Former CIA director John Brennan tweeted that the president's performance in Helsinki "rises to and exceeds the threshold of 'high crimes and misdemeanors.' It was nothing short of treasonous. Not only were Trump's comments imbecilic, he is wholly in the pocket of Putin." Others in Washington and around the country echoed Brennan. "OPEN TREASON," read the *New York Daily News* headline.

Helsinki raises two related questions: Does Trump's capitulation to Putin at Helsinki constitute treason? And does Putin have something on President Trump? When asked at Helsinki whether he had compromising information about President Trump, Putin smiled—one media outlet said "snickered"—but did not deny that he had such information. He said instead that he didn't even know that Trump was in Moscow when he was there in 2013 for the Miss Universe pageant and asked: "Do you think we try to collect compromising information on each and every" visiting American businessperson?

Putin's answer by avoidance—his dangling the possibility that he has compromising information on President Trump—poses a serious question of national security. If Putin has compromising information on President Trump or even if he doesn't and Trump believes he does, we are faced with the specter of an American president who may be subject to blackmail by a hostile foreign power and/or beholden to that power. In these circumstances, would President Trump compromise US interests to protect himself? Where would his allegiance lie?

The Constitution and Treason

Treason is an explosive charge and should not be made lightly. A betrayal of one's own country, it carries the severest of penalties. In the United States, it is both an impeachable offense and a capital crime. The first impeachable offense listed in the Constitution, it is also the only offense to be defined in it: "Treason against the United States shall consist only in levying War against them or in adhering to their Enemies, giving them Aid and Comfort."

Obviously President Trump has not levied war against the United States, but has he satisfied the second prong of the treason test—has he given "aid and comfort to enemies of the United States"?

Though the Constitution does not define "Enemies," the term is generally taken to mean "subjects of a foreign power in a state of open hostility with us." Is Russia an enemy? Russia and the United States are not at war, nor are the two countries in a state of open hostility. On the other hand, isn't a country that has hacked into and attacked our electoral machinery and manipulated social media fighting a twenty-first-century form of war against the United States? Or does the Constitution lock us into the meaning of enemies or war that existed in an era of muskets? There is no clear answer.

President Trump recently gave his opinion on the "enemy" issue at Helsinki. In response to a question, he said that Putin was not an adversary, adding: "I called him a competitor and a good competitor he is. I think the word 'competitor' is a compliment." This is a remarkable assessment of the leader of a country that interfered in our 2016 elections—particularly given that Dan Coats, President Trump's own appointee as director of the Office of National Intelligence, testified that the United States was "under attack" from Russia. The president's opinion, which is not objective, should be disregarded.

Even if we solve the problem of whether Russia is an enemy, has President Trump been "adhering" to Russia? There is no definition of *adhering* in the Constitution, and the most significant definition dates to 1861, when an Ohio district court judge found it "to have no special significance, as the substance is found in the words which follow—giving them aid and comfort." So that takes us to aid and comfort—what does that entail?

The case may be clearer here. President Trump appears to have tried to "deliver" for Russia in a number of ways. He tried to cut back on sanctions imposed by President Barack Obama for election interference and refused to enforce them until the first Mueller indictment. He has continually tried to minimize the seriousness of Russia's interference and even deny its existence, thereby tamping down the likelihood of a much greater enmity to Russia in the public and in Congress. He has stymied implementation of legislation that would require his administration to develop a plan to counter Russia's malign influence. He has given Putin comfort by his generally positive comments about him and by accepting the "sincerity" of Putin's denials of interference when he has every reason to know that they are lies. And some of President Trump's policies—attacking NATO, supporting Brexit, and complimenting the new pro-Russian government in Italy—suggest a disturbing willingness to align himself with Putin. Is this a matter of design or coincidence? Does President Trump's indifference and opposition to election protection reforms meet one of the standards for aid and comfort set by legal scholar Charles Warren—"[a]cts which tend and are designed to defeat, obstruct, or weaken our own arms?" Again, there is no clear answer.

On a different, more practical note, it is important to take account of Supreme Court Chief Justice Salmon Chase's comment on the "odious" nature of treason. He said it points to a general reluctance to lodge the charge against anyone or find that it has been committed. Congress has enacted legislation that deals with treasonous acts, but uses other words and titles to describe them. Similarly, juries may have a disinclination to convict for it. Treason may be so toxic a term and provoke such a strong emotional response with respect to a presidential impeachment that the underlying acts may be less likely to receive the measured attention they deserve.

Even though it might be theoretically possible to make a case for impeaching President Trump on the ground of treason—and much more information would be needed before such a determination were reached—it would be far wiser to forgo that option altogether. The Constitution's treason language, which is based on an English statute dating from 1351 and its encrusted interpretations, makes it very difficult, as we have seen, to apply it to present circumstances.

And there is no need to resort to a charge of treason to find a basis for impeaching President Trump. The constitutional ground of high crimes and misdemeanors should be sufficient to cover any serious, fact-based claim that the president collaborated, conspired, colluded, or worked with Russia to win the 2016 election. That is what we need to turn our attention to.

Other Details regarding Collusion/Conspiracy with Russia

It is important in this regard to consider the large assortment of Trump campaign aides and advisers who had a variety of interactions with the Russian government in connection with the 2016 election. The following review is not meant to be exhaustive, but it points to the possibility of conspiracy or collusion with the Russian government to win the presidency of the United States. If proven, such a conspiracy or such collusion would incontrovertibly be a high crime and misdemeanor, an impeachable offense.

Even though the acts took place prior to Trump's taking office, the debates on the Constitution show that fraud or corruption in securing the presidency would be impeachable. In talking about bribing presidential electors, George Mason posed its need in this regard precisely: "Shall the man who has practised corruption & by that means procured his appointment in the first instance, be suffered to escape punishment, by repeating his guilt?"

The Trump Tower Meeting, WikiLeaks, and "Russia, If You're Listening"

The Trump Tower meeting on June 9, 2016, included President Trump's son Donald Trump Jr.; his son-in-law, Jared Kushner; his campaign manager, Paul Manafort; and five Russians or Russian-connected individuals, among them a lawyer who later admitted having close ties to a high-level Russian official. Although it was initially claimed that the meeting was about Russian adoptions, exposure of Donald Jr.'s emails revealed its true purpose—receipt from the Russians of "incriminating" information about Hillary Clinton. The meeting request specified that this "is part of Russia and its government's support for Mr. Trump." The statement later sent by Donald Jr. to the *New York Times* and putatively written by Donald Jr. suggested, as we have seen, that the president had no knowledge of the meeting.

A central question in an investigation of collusion by President Trump is what he knew of the meeting. President Trump claims he knew nothing of it beforehand, but there are some indications he did know something. Three days prior, on June 6, Donald Jr. had a conversation with a Russian connected to the meeting; he then called a blocked number and later that evening called a blocked number again. He called a blocked number again several hours after the June 9 Trump Tower meeting. Though Donald Trump's former campaign manager said that President Trump had a blocked number, Donald Jr., when asked whether his father had one, incredibly replied: "I don't know."

A second indication came June 7, in a Trump announcement of a "major speech" he would be giving on "probably Monday," June 13, four days after the scheduled meeting: "[W]e're going to be discussing all of the things that have taken place with the Clintons. I think you are going to find it very informative and very, very interesting." While a speech was given, it was not on the expected subject. Was it because the June 9 meeting failed to produce the "incriminating" information that had been promised?

Although both father and son have repeatedly claimed that nothing resulted from the meeting, in an August 2018 tweet President Trump hedged, as we have seen, and in a statement to the *Washington Post* claimed that "to the best of my knowledge, nothing happened after the meeting concluded."

But something did happen after the meeting. Russia promptly took steps to help the Trump campaign. Within five days of the meeting, WikiLeaks announced it was going to release a trove of anti-Clinton material—and made good on its promise about a month later. That material was extremely harmful and disruptive to Democrats, stirring up strong animosity between the Bernie Sanders and Clinton factions.

President Trump has since justified the June 9 meeting repeatedly, stating both that anyone in politics would take a meeting like this to get opposition research and that it was legal. Campaigns do not "take meetings" with just anyone offering opposition research on their opponents, particularly not a foreign government, and generally do not involve the highest-level campaign people when they do. Meetings offering dirt on candidates can easily backfire, as has happened with the Trump Tower meeting. Furthermore, President Trump's claim of legality is incorrect. Federal campaign finance law prohibits both solicitation and acceptance of campaign contributions or things of value from foreigners. "Incriminating" information on Clinton could have been something of value. Thus, if President Trump knew the purpose of the meeting beforehand and gave the go-ahead, or later approved it, he may well have violated federal law, with regard to both campaign finance and collusion.

One further false statement is worth noting. Four months before news of the June 9 meeting broke in 2017, Trump Jr. denied participating in any meetings with Russians related to the campaign. He later had to retract that falsehood.

A second example of possible collusion is Donald Trump's July 27, 2016, press conference statement: "Russia, if you're listening, I hope you're able to find the 30,000 [Hillary Clinton] emails that are missing. . . . I think you will probably be rewarded mightily by our press." Afterward, on that very day, Hillary Clinton's campaign and personal office were subjected to a hacking attempt, the latter for the first time. Trump was publicly calling for illegal activity by a foreign government against his opponent, a former two-term senator and secretary of state. His later walk-back was ludicrous—he claimed he meant that the found emails should be turned over by Russia to the FBI. It is preposterous to think that he wanted Russia to commit computer-tampering crimes and then cooperate with the FBI. Was Russia's hacking in response to Trump's urging, or was it a coincidence?

Candidate Trump also repeatedly saluted WikiLeaks for releasing the Podesta emails, thus likely encouraging and supporting criminal activity by a foreign government and its apparent agent. WikiLeaks, which "the American intelligence community believes was chosen by the Russian government to disseminate the information it had hacked," according to the *Atlantic*, continued to release the Podesta information. Was that due to Trump's encouragement, or was it a coincidence?

The release of the *Access Hollywood* tape that records President Trump bragging about sexually assaulting women again raises a question of collusion. It threatened to bury the Trump campaign. An hour after the public began hearing the tape, WikiLeaks initiated a slow-motion release over several weeks of the John Podesta emails, diverting attention from what would otherwise have been an overwhelmingly negative story for Trump. Was this a result of savvy political instincts on the part of Russian military intelligence or WikiLeaks, was it a coincidence, or was it a result of coordination with the Trump campaign?

If Russia's actions were taken in response to requests from or in coordination with Trump or his campaign, a matter that would have to be established, then the possibility of a high crime or misdemeanor looms large.

Connections Between Top Campaign Aides and Advisers and Russia

Roger Stone, a self-confessed "dirty trickster" who began his career in President Nixon's 1972 reelection campaign and later partnered with Paul Manafort in a lobbying firm, had been advising Donald Trump to run for president since 1988 and was his top adviser during the first Republican presidential debates. He was dismissed in August 2015 but reportedly continued to be in communication with the candidate.

Stone had a number of extremely problematic contacts during the campaign with Guccifer 2.0, the pseudonym, as we have seen, for one or more of Russia's military intelligence officers. On August 8, 2016, at a speech in Florida, Stone answered a question about whether Julian Assange would produce an October Surprise to affect the election: "I actually have communicated with Assange. I believe the next tranche of his documents pertain to the Clinton Foundation, but there's no telling what the October Surprise may be." Guccifer 2.0, as we have seen, delivered the hacked DNC emails to WikiLeaks. Did Stone keep candidate Trump advised of his interactions with Guccifer and Assange?

Three days before that speech, a Stone essay on Breitbart.com claimed Guccifer 2.0 as the lone hacker responsible for the DNC hack, not the Russians. When Twitter suspended Guccifer 2.0's account for releasing personal information about Democrats in the House of Representatives, Stone called Twitter's action "outrageous." He declared Guccifer 2.0 a "HERO" in a tweet and later applauded Twitter's restoration of Guccifer 2.0's account: "Thank you Sweet Jesus. I've prayed for it." Guccifer 2.0 responded to Stone, saying, "thanks that u believe in the real #Guccifer2."

Then Guccifer 2.0 showed gratitude by promoting a link to Roger Stone's article about how the election might be rigged against Donald Trump. Guccifer 2.0 explained the action as "paying u back." Stone and Guccifer 2.0, respectively a Trump adviser and Russian military intelligence officer(s), were helping and praising each other, communicating at some point directly through Twitter's Direct Messages portal (although it is not clear that all the messages have been made public). Guccifer 2.0 at one point tweeted Stone: "I'm pleased to say that u r a great man. . . . please tell me if I can help u anyhow. It would be a great pleasure to me."

Stone also appeared to know beforehand that Clinton's campaign chair John Podesta's emails were going to be released through WikiLeaks ("it will soon [be] Podesta's time in the barrel," he tweeted on August 21, 2016). In an interview with a right-wing site, Stone again stated that he had interacted with Assange.

For Stone's contacts with Guccifer 2.0 and Assange to form a basis for impeachment, we would need to know whether Stone was acting on behalf of the campaign or Donald Trump, whether Stone advised Trump or the campaign of these contacts, and whether Stone realized the Russia connection. These and other questions are now in the hands of special counsel Mueller, and Stone himself has raised the possibility that he might be indicted.

Michael Flynn, President Trump's national security adviser, pleaded guilty in late 2017 to lying to the FBI about whether he discussed sanctions with Russian ambassador Sergey Kislyak. The first discussion took place on December 28–29, 2016, and concerned the fact that "'members of the [Trump] transition team" do not want Russia to escalate," according to a *New York Times* timeline of Russian election interference. It was on the twenty-ninth that President Obama ejected thirty-five Russian diplomats and announced that he was imposing sanctions for Russia's interference in the presidential election. The second discussion was on December 31. Flynn was a member of Trump's transition team at the time. Kislyak told Flynn that "Russia chose not to retaliate in response to Flynn's request." In essence, then, the focus of the discussions was that Trump might look at sanctions differently and that Russia should not overreact. Flynn's messages were apparently delivered to President Putin, who responded as requested. He announced that Russia would not take retaliatory actions against the United States, a decision hailed by President-elect Trump between the two discussions. "Great move on delay (by V Putin)," he tweeted on December 30. "I always knew he was very smart!"

A series of denials followed. Flynn falsely denied to the FBI that he had discussed sanctions with Kislyak. Members of the incoming Trump administration denied they'd ever spoken among themselves about sanctions. Vice

President Mike Pence denied five days before the inauguration that Flynn's conversations with Kislyak concerned sanctions.

Then came the firings: Six days after President Trump was sworn in, acting attorney general Sally Yates advised the White House of FBI evidence that Flynn was lying, and that his compromised position left him dangerously open to blackmail by the Russian government. Four days later she was fired, and within two weeks Flynn was gone.

Why was the discussion of sanctions something to conceal? Did Flynn know about Russian help during the campaign and the campaign's efforts to get it? If the lie was intended to cover up a deal with Russia involving election help from Russia in exchange for relief on sanctions, it could lay the foundation for an impeachable offense. Flynn's actions both during the campaign and after would have to be examined in great detail to determine if collusion occurred.

George Papadopoulos, a foreign affairs adviser to the Trump campaign, pleaded guilty in October 2017 to lying to the FBI about his ties to Russia. Records show that he was in frequent touch with Michael Flynn and Trump campaign chief Steve Bannon regarding his efforts to broker ties with the Russian government. Hearing from a man he later identified as a European professor that the Russians had dirt on Hillary Clinton, he transmitted this information to several people in the Trump campaign.

Why did Papadopoulos lie? What was there to conceal? We need to know more about both Papadopoulos's effort to create ties between the Trump campaign and Russia and how the "dirt on Hillary" information was handled by the campaign, including whether Trump himself was informed.

Carter Page, another foreign affairs adviser to the campaign, met with top officials in Russia and was a target of the Russian government's spy recruitment effort. Page was already well known to American intelligence for his Russian sympathies—and was praised on Russian state television as a "famous American economist." US intelligence officials obtained wiretaps on Page, which were approved by the special foreign intelligence surveillance court. When word emerged of alleged contacts between Page and Russian officials, including the president of Rosneft, a state-run oil conglomerate, Page resigned. Trump campaign communications director said of Page, "He's never been part of our campaign. Period." Five months earlier, in the same press interview in which he discussed Papadopoulos, Trump acknowledged Page as an "excellent guy." Page's interactions with the Russians would need further probing.

The Steele dossier, officially titled "Trump-Russia Dossier," reported many connections. The one that caught the public imagination was his suggestion that Putin had *kompromat* on Trump—specifically, that he consorted with prostitutes in Moscow. It also claimed that Michael Cohen, Trump's personal lawyer and fixer, had traveled to Prague to arrange for a new liaison to the Russians on election interference after Trump campaign manager Paul Manafort resigned. It alleged that Cohen had discussed trying to destroy evidence of any connection between the Russian agents and the Trump campaign if Clinton won.

If Cohen traveled to Prague and met with Russian officials to coordinate Russian campaign assistance, as the dossier claimed, and if candidate Trump knew of his activities, it would likely support not only impeachment charges, but criminal ones as well. More information needs to be developed about this. It would also seem critical to verify/disprove the *kompromat* allegation: if President Trump is being blackmailed by Putin, impeachment may be an urgent remedy.

After an investigation by New York–based federal prosecutors, Cohen pleaded guilty to eight federal charges of tax violations and bank fraud. Two of the charges related to hush-money payments Cohen claimed were directed by Trump, which are discussed below. Cohen has since been talking to prosecutors on Mueller's team.

The National Rifle Association may also figure in the Russian interference matter. Donald Trump Jr. met with a top Russian oligarch, Alexander Torshin, at an NRA convention in May, 2016. Reportedly close to Putin, Torshin was suspected by Spanish authorities of involvement with Russian organized crime syndicates. He was also close to Maria Butina, the subject of the July 2018 indictment in the Russian election interference investigation for allegedly being an unregistered Russian agent. Press reports suggest that Torshin may have used Butina to funnel millions of dollars to the National Rifle Association money for use in supporting the Trump campaign.

More needs to be uncovered about this matter. But, if the Trump campaign was aware of the Russian campaign contribution and nonetheless accepted support from the NRA, it could spell trouble for the Trump campaign, and, depending on his personal knowledge, for President Trump himself—not to mention the NRA.

Grounds for Impeachment

As we have seen, the first question about Trump's conduct is whether under the Constitution a president may be impeached for actions taken before he or she is sworn into office. In other words, may President Trump be impeached for conspiring with Russia during his campaign for the presidency?

As noted above, George Mason was clear about the matter at the Constitutional Convention. Professor Laurence Tribe and Joshua Matz, in *To End a Presidency*, support and explain Mason's position: "Without an impeachment process, presidents could obtain office corruptly and then enjoy the poisonous fruit of their own electoral treachery. Democracy itself might be destroyed."

Under Mason's doctrine, if Trump conspired, colluded, or collaborated with the Russian government to obtain its help in damaging his opponent and advancing his candidacy to win the election, he could be subject to impeachment for it. Events occurring before taking office may create a basis for removal from office when those events are related to the fraudulent or corrupt acquisition of office. Collusion with Russia to secure the presidency would fit this requirement. Moreover, aspects of the possible Russian collusion have migrated into the Trump presidency. We see it in the president's inexplicable support for Russia, his cover-up of Russian connections with his campaign, and his attacks on the Mueller investigation into them.

Is there sufficient information available to impeach Trump for colluding/conspiring with Russia?

The information currently available shows an intense desire on the part of the Trump campaign and people associated with it to secure Russian aid in the election. We know the willingness and intent to receive information in the instance of the Trump Tower meeting, also a likely violation of federal campaign finance law. We know of the specific request by candidate Trump for Russian help in finding the Hillary Clinton emails, made at his July 27, 2016, press conference. The same day, there was a Russian response: an attempt by GRU hackers to access Hillary Clinton emails, followed by a WikiLeaks announcement of their forthcoming release. (Hacked DNC emails had been released by WikiLeaks July 22.)

But there are some critical missing elements. We do not know for certain that Donald Trump knew about the Trump Tower meeting beforehand, and we do not know whether Russia's actions in trying to hack Clinton on the same day that Trump called for it was in response to Trump's appeal or if the WikiLeaks announcement was in response to the June 9 meeting.

We also know of Trump's personal encouragement of hacking, in the Clinton and Podesta examples, and of the response as well—the continued release of emails by WikiLeaks. We know that Trump confidant Roger Stone was in contact with Russian spies and encouraged them to continue their work. But did he know they were Russian? Or spies? Was he acting on behalf of the campaign? Did Trump know about the contacts and approve?

The large number of contacts between the Russian government and the Trump campaign is certainly troublesome, and the lies about these contacts suggest that there is something to hide. The continued cover-up of Russia's involvement in the election carries the assault on our democracy into Trump's presidency. Further troubling are the concerns raised by Trump's policies that mirror Putin's objectives, such as Trump's attacks on NATO.

While Mueller is pursuing whether some of the actions of Trump and his campaign related to Russia are indictable, the question for us is if they are impeachable. The only way to ascertain this is by serious investigation. It needn't occur in the context of an impeachment inquiry, but it is imperative to determine whether there is just a lot of smoke or if there is fire, too. Not only national but international security may depend on it.

Some Historical Perspective on Foreign Collusion: The Nixon Precedent

If Donald Trump colluded with Russia to get elected, it would not be the first time in American history that a presidential candidate covertly worked with a foreign power to affect the outcome of an election. It happened with President Richard Nixon. The issue of treachery should have been part of the House Judiciary Committee's impeachment proceedings against him, and he should have been charged with betraying his country, but there was not a hint of that subject in the proceedings. The facts just weren't known then. Nixon biographer John A. Farrell put together the elusive pieces of the puzzle and wrote about the matter in *Politico* in 2014 and later in his *Richard Nixon: The Life*.

In late October 1968, just before the presidential election, President Lyndon Johnson called a bombing halt in Vietnam to allow peace talks to take place in Paris. The time was propitious for a settlement of the war, since the Russians were pushing for it, too. Nixon, the Republican candidate, got wind of the peace efforts and became frightened that a peace treaty would help his Democratic opponent win the election. He wanted to sabotage, or as he put it, "monkey wrench" the peace talks, according to notes taken by his top aide, H. R. Haldeman.

Nixon personally directed that a "back channel" to the South Vietnamese government be used. That channel was Anna Chennault, a fixture on the Washington scene and a top Republican fund-raiser who had been married to a US general stationed in China during World War II. As instructed, she contacted South Vietnam's US ambassador and told him to "hold on. We are gonna win." She was urging the South Vietnamese not to sign any peace agreement because Nixon was going to win the election and give South Vietnam a better deal than it could get under President Johnson. The plan worked. Several days later, South Vietnam announced it was boycotting the Paris peace talks. The peace initiative was dead, and Nixon won the presidency.

President Johnson knew of Chennault's phone conversation because the FBI monitored it. He called it "treason" in a private talk with Republican senator Everett Dirksen, who agreed with him. President Johnson did not make the matter public, and Nixon's direct role was unknown until Farrell found Haldeman's notes a few years ago. The Chennault phone call may have postponed the end of the Vietnam War for five years. During that time, 20,000 American soldiers died, as did large numbers of Vietnamese soldiers and civilians, untold numbers were injured, and great destruction and devastation continued to take place.

We should not have to wait fifty years to learn whether Trump conspired with Russia—and we will not have to if a serious and thorough inquiry on that question is undertaken. If it turns out that there was no conspiracy—just a great deal of evocative suggestions of one—so much the better. If a conspiracy occurred, though, we need to know it so that we can protect the country by removing the president from office.

ABUSE OF POWER BY SEPARATING CHILDREN FROM PARENTS

After assuming office, as part of his anti-immigration policy, President Trump initiated a policy to reduce the influx of people, including refugees, from the Central American countries of Guatemala, El Salvador, and Honduras (the "Northern Triangle"). Their journey is often a treacherous one through Mexico, with serious dangers encountered along the way. While some cross the US border simply to seek economic opportunity, many, often single mothers, come with their children fleeing serious violence by gangs or others in their home countries. Some apply for asylum once they reach the United States and seek refugee status.

From July to November 2017, the Trump administration began testing in a limited geographical area a new approach: separating children and parents at the border. This was a shock and awe operation: seize the children and thus terrify and traumatize parents who would get word back to the Northern Triangle that children would be forcibly taken away if they tried to enter the United States with their parents.

Whatever the results of that pilot effort, it was clear that by May 2018, a large-scale program of child separation had been put into place across the Southwest border of the United States, under which children were taken from their parents by Department of Homeland Security personnel and placed in the custody of the State Department's Office of Refugee Resettlement. There was no room for discretion or compassion of any kind. Infants and toddlers, disabled and sick children were also taken, sometimes under false pretenses and sometimes by force. Many parents were not given an opportunity to say good-bye. Many didn't understand what was happening: there were acute language difficulties because many didn't speak Spanish, but only indigenous languages. Many were told untruths about what was happening. Worst of all, in many cases the parents were not given any information about how to find their child or children, nor did the federal government take appropriate information from the separated children to identify them or their parents to ensure reunification. And hundreds of parents were deported without their children, ensuring great difficulties in reunification. In some cases, the taking of children was used as a threat to force parents to give up their asylum claim.

According to a DHS report of June 16, 2018, 2,342 children were separated from adults on the border between May 5 and June 9 alone. Lawsuits were brought to stop the program and secure reunification—one by the attorneys general of seventeen states and the District of Columbia. That suit claimed the Trump administration "made clear that the purpose of separating families is not to protect children, but rather to create a public spectacle designed to deter potential immigrants from coming to the United States."

The impetus for this program was President Trump's personal frustration with the increased influx over the Southwest border, and he was the one who issued orders to the attorney general and the secretary of the Department of

Homeland Security to address the problem. One of those directives dealt with ending the so-called catch and release program, which had allowed the release of families with children after they turned themselves over to or were apprehended by federal authorities.

After a huge public outcry excoriating the separation policy, President Trump referred to the policy in a May 26, 2018, tweet as a "horrible law." He signed an executive order on June 20, 2018, purporting to end it. No provision, however, was made to reunite families. It took an order from a federal court to force the president and his administration to start the process. Under court supervision, many families were reunified, though not all. Months after the order, more than 500 children were still not reunited with their families, quite possibly because, as reported by the *New York Times*, more than 300 parents were deported without their children. Locating them has been an exceedingly difficult task that has fallen to private organizations. In addition to the language barriers, some parents live in very remote areas in the Northern Triangle and are very poor, without phones or Internet.

Abundant evidence of the harm inflicted by this separation policy has been gathered. Press reports based on interviews with parents who were reunited with their children after weeks of separation show various kinds of serious psychological trauma to the children. Experts have stated that the harm could be long-lasting, even permanent. If serious damage was apparent in the children who were reunited after only weeks of separation, think of the damage still being done to those children who have not yet been reunited.

According to a statement released by Dr. Colleen Kraft, president of the American Academy of Pediatrics, which strongly opposed the child separation policy: "In fact, highly stressful experiences, like family separation, can cause irreparable harm, disrupting a child's brain architecture and affecting his or her health. This type of prolonged exposure to serious stress—known as toxic stress—can carry lifelong consequences for children." The statement is used as supporting evidence in a federal class-action lawsuit filed September 5, 2018, against the administration, seeking monetary damage for trauma inflicted. More harm was described by Dr. Kraft, who visited a detention facility for children. There she saw a girl, less than two years old, who was screaming; because shelter workers had been prohibited from touching or holding the child, the child could not be comforted.

Separating children from parents is a lawless policy. There is nothing in US immigration law that authorizes taking children from parents as a penalty for violation of immigration laws. In imposing such a penalty, therefore,

President Trump abuses the power of his office in a most serious way. Taking children from parents (when done not to protect the child) is not just "horrible," as he himself has said. It is cruel, depraved, merciless. Yet, without lawful authority, the president has directed and approved what amounts to the kidnapping and torture of thousands of children. No concern for family reunification was apparent at any stage in the policy's implementation. The children and parents targeted, probably because of their Latin American origin, were not even viewed as human.

Furthermore, it appears that one of President Trump's motives in creating this "horrible" program was to force the Democrats to accept his immigration policies, including building his wall. He all but admitted this on June 16, 2018: "Democrats can fix their forced family breakup at the Border by working with Republicans on new legislation." A lawsuit filed by the state attorneys general against the administration decried this approach: "[F]amilies are intentionally being traumatized for political gain." The separation of children from parents for political gain is a great and dangerous offense.

There are other serious constitutional issues involved in the policy. Significantly, it was put into effect only on the Southwest border, where most border crossers are Hispanic. President Trump's hostility to Hispanics is well known. He characterized Mexicans as "rapists" during his campaign, called El Salvador a "shithole country," and in May 2018 said of undocumented immigrants from Central America and Mexico: "You wouldn't believe how bad these people are. These aren't people. These are animals." Imposing a program of separating children from parents on a racial or ethnic basis is an abuse of power, and it also violates the constitutional rights of the children and parents to equal protection of the law. Absent evidence that being together is harmful, it is also a violation of due process to separate children and parents without a court hearing of any kind.

President Trump's indifference to basic legal norms and his willingness to abandon due process are deeply rooted. On June 21 and 24, 2018, the president proposed that immigrants who cross the border be sent back without an opportunity for court appearance. "When somebody comes in, we must immediately, with no Judges or Court Cases, bring them back from where they came," he tweeted on June 25.

A president who so deliberately, cruelly, and casually inflicted serious mental and psychological harm on thousands, manifestly on an ethnic basis, as a deterrent to others and as a political tool to get legislation passed without regard to the rights of the children and parents, has subverted the

Constitution. He poses a direct and immediate threat to the rule of law. Watergate set the precedent for concluding that these acts could form grounds for impeachment.

President Nixon was charged with high crimes and misdemeanors because his acts were an egregious abuse of power and violated the constitutional rights of Americans. Two specific examples of this are the illegal break-in into Daniel Ellsberg's psychiatrist's office and the illegal wiretapping of journalists and White House staffers. The lawless policy of separating children at the border had thousands more victims and inflicted much more serious and possibly long-lasting mental harm on them. Because the policy is also subversive of the Constitution and is as serious an assault on constitutional rights as President Nixon committed, it may well be a high crime and misdemeanor and may form the basis of an article of impeachment against President Trump.

Campaign Finance Law Violations

Donald Trump and former Playboy model Karen McDougal allegedly had an affair in 2006 and 2007. McDougal was interested in publishing a story about that affair prior to the 2106 presidential election. In the summer of 2016, as a result of the efforts of Trump's personal lawyer and fixer Michael Cohen, American Media, Inc. (AMI), the parent company of the *National Enquirer*, paid $150,000 to McDougal for rights to her story. AMI had no intention of publishing the story. Its object—and Michael Cohen's—was to bury the story and make sure it never saw the light of day.

Donald Trump and Stephanie Clifford, better known by her adult film name Stormy Daniels, allegedly had an affair in 2006, four months after Trump's wife Melania gave birth to their son. Shortly before the presidential election in November 2016, Daniels was paid $130,000 in hush money not to reveal the alleged Trump affair. Cohen was the intermediary. Trump later admitted reimbursing Cohen for the Daniels payment.

In January 2018, the *Wall Street Journal* broke the details of the Daniels payment, with a quote from Cohen that President-elect Trump "vehemently denies any such occurrence." Less than two weeks later, a watchdog group filed a complaint with the Federal Election Commission and DOJ asking them to "determine whether the payment was made by the Trump Organization or some other corporation or individual, which would [make] it an illegal in-kind contribution to the campaign." Corporations, under federal law, are not permitted to donate to candidates, and individual contributions, except by candidates to themselves, are capped at $2,700 for a general election.

On August 21, 2018, Cohen pleaded guilty in federal court to tax evasion and bank fraud. Most explosive were two counts involved violating campaign finance law. Cohen pleaded guilty to making an illegal, excessive campaign contribution to Daniels and to causing an unlawful corporate contribution during the 2016 election by helping AMI in connection with buying the McDougal story.

In court, Cohen described the two instances of election-law violations. In essence, he claimed that Trump had directed his actions to buy silence from McDougal and Daniels. With regard to McDougal, he admitted that "in coordination with, and at the direction of, a candidate for federal office [Donald Trump] I and the CEO of a media company [AMI] at the request of the candidate worked together to keep an individual with information that would be harmful to the candidate and to the campaign from publicly disclosing this information." The media company entered "into a contract with the individual under which she received compensation of $150,000."

With respect to Daniels, he admitted that a shell company he had created two weeks earlier made the $130,000 payment "in coordination with and at the direction of [Donald Trump]. . . . The information would be harmful to the candidate and to the campaign" and the payment was made "to keep the individual from disclosing the information." The actions were undertaken, Cohen's plea specified, "for the principal purpose of influencing the election."

ARE THESE IMPEACHABLE OFFENSES?

The issue is whether candidate Trump's actions amount to high crimes or misdemeanors. More information would be needed to make that determination. Do we know, for example, what candidate Trump's motives were—to affect the election by concealing harmful information, or to protect his wife and his family from hurtful information? Does it matter if he had a mixed motive?

President Trump also denies that he directed Cohen's actions, though Cohen's claim that he did was made to a judge under penalty of perjury. Even if we assume that the alleged affairs happened, that candidate Trump knew all the facts beforehand, and that he directed Cohen to pay hush money and to coordinate with AMI, does this justify impeachment?

The payment of hush money has superficial resemblances to Watergate. There, Nixon used his personal lawyer, Herbert Kalmbach, to pay hush money to the Watergate burglars to ensure their silence before the election. The hush money was critical to President Nixon's reelection, and President Nixon knew it would be—and the payment of hush money was one of the grounds for Nixon's impeachment. Kalmbach was convicted of a crime in connection with the payoffs.

There is no question that Trump's conduct is slimy and sleazy and may involve a possible criminal violation of election laws. As we know from Watergate, however, not every criminal violation of the law by a president is a high crime or misdemeanor—and even those that are do not necessarily warrant impeachment. Nixon's tax issues, with the possibility of tax fraud, are good examples. The House Judiciary Committee did not vote for impeachment on that ground.

The seriousness of President Trump's behavior relates to his effort to conceal his adulterous behavior from the American people right before an election. The campaign law violations kept the hush-money payments and Trump's role in them secret. Trump also apparently has lied to the public about his involvement with these women in order to advance his candidacy.

At the present moment, it does not appear that the hush-money payments themselves are egregious enough or pose a sufficiently grave danger to the rule of law to warrant impeachment.

Unlike in Watergate, the hush payments here were not made to cover up a crime—a critical distinction, although crimes were committed in connection with making the payments. As with Watergate, however, the cover-up may have had a determinative effect on Trump's election to the presidency. An impeachment inquiry may want to examine this in greater depth, particularly since some individuals related to the matter are being questioned by prosecutors, and more and different information damaging to the president or exonerative of him may emerge.

Conclusion

Donald Trump is a clear and present danger to our democracy. I have shown evidence of how he appears to have assaulted the rule of law in deep and serious ways. Whether it is his effort to impede and obstruct the investigations into Russian interference, his refusal to protect our election system from Russian manipulation, his open hand to payments his businesses receive from foreign governments and domestically, or his assault on the rights of thousands of children at the border, the president's misdeeds cast a wide net. They are ongoing, with no end in sight. And he continues to spin a web of incessant and brazen falsehoods, deceptions, and lies to disguise and conceal the misdeeds.

In 1973, the country also faced a president run amok. Richard Nixon, whose campaign minions broke into the Watergate complex, orchestrated a vast, multipronged effort to stymie investigations into the burglary. Nixon engaged in other nefarious activities and abuses of power: he violated the rights of Americans though illegal wiretaps of journalists, an illegal break-in into a psychiatrist's office for damaging information, an order for IRS audits of political opponents—the Enemies List—to name a few.

Nixon's cover-up was effective: it got him reelected with one of the largest electoral margins in American history. Then, it began to unravel. Evidence harmful to him came to light, and, in a grandiose move of maximum presidential authority, he ordered the special prosecutor investigating him to be fired. That's where the American people drew the line. They demanded that Congress take action, and it did. It started an inquiry, which resulted in a bipartisan vote for articles of impeachment, forcing Nixon to resign.

It was in response to obstruction that the articles of impeachment against Nixon were adopted. Their message? Presidents cannot block, tamper with, and destroy the machinery of justice that is aimed at them. If they do, it is at their peril. They face impeachment, removal from office, even imprisonment. But if *we* allow presidents to block, tamper with, and destroy the machinery of justice that is aimed at them, *we* do so at our peril. The rule of law will go up in smoke. We will enshrine two standards of justice, one for the powerful and one for everyone else. We will find ourselves on the road to tyranny.

It is a road that we're dangerously close to traveling today.

Nixon worked mightily to stop the institutions of justice from closing in on him and his associates. So has President Trump. Not every aspect of Nixon's impeachable offenses is replicated in President Trump's behavior. Still, there are astonishing and troublesome parallels, particularly in the Russia investigation, including Trump's firing the FBI director (Nixon had the special Watergate prosecutor fired); dangling pardon possibilities to those under investigation (Nixon did the same); making relentless and false attacks on the investigation and those conducting it (Nixon called for an end to the investigations and engaged in other attacks); and deceiving the public and Congress constantly and systematically (Nixon did that, too).

Watergate started with burglars who used burglars' tools to break into the Democratic National Committee headquarters at the Watergate Hotel complex in Washington, DC. They were interfering in the 1972 presidential election. The investigation of Donald Trump started with the Russians' using cyber tools to break into the DNC computer servers and interfere in the 2016 presidential election. We don't know what the Watergate burglars were looking for. We don't know what the Russians' real objective was, or even the full impact of their interference. It may even have vaulted Donald Trump into the White House.

But we do know that Trump called for Russian help in winning the election. And we know that Russia gave him help.

Was the help coordinated with the Trump campaign or just coincidental? If coordinated, then Trump has committed a high crime and misdemeanor of the gravest kind—working with an unfriendly foreign power in violation of our campaign finance and other laws to get elected. It is imperative for Congress to ascertain the facts, and not leave us to speculate or with a secretly beholden president.

Trump's effort to block the investigation into his possible collusion with the Russians over the 2016 election on the face of it warrants an impeachment inquiry. It may well be that a full examination of his behavior will exonerate him, but, given the record of his tweets and his public statements, not to mention his firing of FBI director James Comey, it is more likely that his actions have been prompted by the impermissible and impeachable objective of stopping the investigations before they find him out.

President Trump's misconduct does not stop with his repeated attempts to impede the Russia investigations. He has steadfastly refused to protect our election system from further Russian attack, failing to fulfill his central obligation as president to take care that the laws be faithfully executed. This failure too is related to his effort to impede the Russia investigation. If the American people, including his "base," fully understood the seriousness and scope of the Russian attacks, they would demand effective measures from the president to stop them, but they also might question why President Trump is calling the investigation a hoax when the Russians really attacked us, as our intelligence agencies, the Justice Department, and private social media companies have found.

The president has also defied and flouted the Constitution's ban on emoluments on a very large scale, creating the appearance if not the reality of influence peddling at the highest level of our government. This is another assault on our democracy.

Finally, President Trump's lawless and heartless separation of thousands of children from parents on the Southwest border is an action that violates our Constitution's deepest promises of due process and equal protection. The willingness to assault the Constitution by harming so many threatens all of us.

President Trump's misconduct continues and expands. He has relentlessly attacked the press, undermining public confidence in it and charging that it is an enemy of the people, despite its central importance to our democracy, which is enshrined in the first amendment to the Constitution. He has divided the country, attacking women's rights and the rights of African Americans and Hispanics, not to mention the rights of immigrants/refugees and others entering the United States, and fostered bigotry by mimicking a victim of sexual assault, calling for the firing of NFL players who have kneeled to protest the shooting of black young men in America, and equating neo-Nazis with civil rights activists. Not any of these acts is impeachable, but they illuminate a presidency without respect for diversity—whether of opinion, race, ethnicity, or gender.

Together, President Trump's actions are indicative of a president who has established a different standard of justice for himself—exactly the kind that we declared impermissible in Nixon's articles of impeachment. He has done so at the expense of democracy. And he's done so at his own peril.

There is a remedy—and I participated in it and lived through it and saw it work. The solution is what Congress, the courts, and the press used in dealing with President Nixon in Watergate. It means imposing accountability and holding the president to the rule of law, as we did then.

In Watergate, there was a criminal investigation and there were congressional inquiries, including an impeachment process. All were thorough and fair; all won the respect of the public. And together they reestablished the public's faith in the viability of our democracy and the Constitution.

No one, not even a president, is above the law. That is the lesson of Watergate, and it must continue to be the lesson today.

Now we face the same pivotal moment. If we tolerate a president who wants to smash the criminal justice system that is trying to hold him accountable and part ways with other legal norms, we are well on the path to seeing the precious, fragile constitutional system that was passed on to us pass through our fingers. We dare not let that happen.

Today we have the advantage of knowing what to do, of having the model for action—full throated congressional inquiries, a bipartisan impeachment inquiry, and an investigation by Robert Mueller that proceeds without interference until it is properly concluded. These are simple, realizable objectives.

The American people can force action on this agenda as they did in response to presidential misconduct in Watergate. We have the power, we have the votes. We are still a democracy. If this book tells us anything, it is that we will have to fight hard, really hard, to keep it that way. And we can.

APPENDIX I

Report on the History and Law
of Impeachments

In February 1974, the House Judiciary Committee released a report on the history and law of impeachments. The following excerpts contain the report's summary of the key constitutional impeachment provisions and the history of the Impeachment Clause's adoption at the Constitutional Convention.

CONSTITUTIONAL GROUNDS FOR PRESIDENTIAL IMPEACHMENT
REPORT BY THE STAFF OF THE IMPEACHMENT INQUIRY

Introduction

The Constitution deals with the subject of impeachment and conviction at six places. The scope of the power is set out in Article II, Section 4:

The President, Vice President and all civil Officers of the United States, shall be removed from Office on Impeachment for, and Conviction of, Treason, Bribery, or other high Crimes and Misdemeanors.

Other provisions deal with procedures and consequences.

Article I, Section 2:

The House of Representatives . . . shall have the sole Power of Impeachment.
    Similarly, Article I, Section 3, describes the Senate's role:
    The Senate shall have the sole Power to try all Impeachments. When sitting for that Purpose, they shall be on Oath or Affirmation. When the President of the United States is tried, the Chief Justice shall preside: And no

Person shall be convicted without the Concurrence of two thirds of the Members present.

The same section limits the consequences of judgement in cases of impeachment:

Judgement in Cases of Impeachment shall not extend further than to removal from Office, and disqualification to hold and enjoy any Office of honor, Trust or Profit under the United States: but the Party convicted shall nevertheless be liable and subject to Indictment, Trial, Judgement and Punishment, according to Law.

Of lesser significance, although mentioning the subject, are: Article II, Section 2:

The President . . . shall have Power to grant Reprieves and Pardons for Offenses against the United States, except in Cases of Impeachment.

Article III, Section 2:

The Trial of all Crimes, except in Cases of Impeachment, shall be by Jury . . .

. . .

Delicate issues of basic constitutional law are involved. Those issues cannot be defined in detail in advance of full investigation of the facts. The Supreme Court of the United States does not reach out, in the abstract, to rule on the constitutionality of statutes or of conduct. Cases must be brought and adjudicated on particular facts in terms of the Constitution. Similarly, the House does not engage in abstract advisory or hypothetical debates about the precise nature of conduct that calls for the exercise of its constitutional powers; rather it must await full development of the facts and understanding of the events to which those facts relate.

What is said here does not reflect any prejudgement of the facts or any opinion or inference respecting the allegations being investigated. This memorandum is written before completion of the full and fair factual investigation the House directed be undertaken. It is intended to be a review of the precedents and available interpretive materials, seeking general principles to guide the Committee.

This memorandum offers no fixed standards for determining whether grounds for impeachment exist. The framers did not write a fixed standard. Instead they adopted from English history a standard sufficiently general and flexible to meet future circumstances and events, the nature and character of which they could not foresee.

The House has set in motion an unusual constitutional process, conferred solely upon it by the Constitution, by directing the Judiciary Committee to "investigate fully and completely whether sufficient grounds exist for the House of Representatives to exercise its constitutional power to impeach." This action was not partisan. It was supported by the overwhelming majority of both political parties. Nor was it intended to obstruct or weaken presidency. It was supported by Members firmly committed to the need for a strong presidency and a healthy executive branch of our government. The House of Representatives acted out of a clear sense of constitutional duty to resolve issues of a kind that more familiar constitutional processes are unable to restore.

To assist the Committee in working toward that resolution, this memorandum reports upon the history, purpose and meaning of the constitutional phrase, "Treason, Bribery, or other high Crimes and Misdemeanors."

. . .

The Intentions of the Framers

The debates on impeachment at the Constitutional Convention in Philadelphia focus principally on its applicability to the President. The framers sought to create a responsible though strong executive; they hoped, in the words of Elbridge Gerry of Massachusetts, that "the maxim would never be adopted here that the chief Magistrate could do [no] wrong." Impeachment was to be one of the central elements of executive responsibility in the framework of the new government as they conceived it.

The constitutional grounds for impeachment of the President received little direct attention in the Convention; the phrase "other high Crimes and Misdemeanors" was ultimately added to "Treason" and "Bribery" with virtually no debate. There is evidence, however, that the framers were aware of the technical meaning the phrase had acquired in English impeachments. Ratification by nine states was required to convert the Constitution from a proposed plan of government to the supreme law of the land. The public debates in the state ratifying conventions offer evidence of the contemporaneous understanding of the Constitution equally as compelling as the secret deliberations of the delegates in Philadelphia. That evidence, together with the evidence found in the debates during the First Congress on the power of the President to discharge an executive officer appointed with the advice and consent of the Senate, shows that the framers intended impeachment to be a constitutional safeguard of the public trust, the powers of government conferred upon the President and other civil officers, and the division of powers among the legislative, judicial and executive departments.

1. The Purpose of the Impeachment Remedy

Among the weaknesses of the Articles of Confederation apparent to the delegates to the Constitutional Convention was that they provided for a purely legislative form of government whose ministers were subservient to Congress. One of the first decisions of the delegates was that their new plan should included a separate executive, judiciary, and legislature. However, the framers sought to avoid the creation of a too-powerful executive. The Revolution had been fought against the tyranny of a king and his council, and the framers sought to build in safeguards against executive abuse and usurpation of power. They explicitly rejected a plural executive, despite arguments that they were creating "the foetus of monarchy," because a single person would give the most responsibility to the office. For the same reason, they rejected proposals for a council of advice or privy council to the executive.

The provision for single executive was vigorously defended at the time of the state ratifying conventions as a protection against executive tyranny and wrongdoing. Alexander Hamilton made the most carefully reasoned argument in *Federalist* No. 70, one of the series of *Federalist* papers prepared to advocate the ratification of the Constitution by the State of New York. Hamilton criticized both a plural executive and a council because they tend "to conceal faults and destroy responsibility." A plural executive, he wrote, deprives the people of "the two greatest securities they can have for the faithful exercise of any delegated power"—"[r]esponsibility . . . to censure and to punishment." When censure is divided and responsibility uncertain, "the restraints of public opinion . . . lose their efficacy" and "the opportunity of discovering with facility and clearness the misconduct of the persons [the public] trust, in order either to their removal from office, or to their actual punishment in cases which admit of it" is lost. A council, too, "would serve to destroy, or would greatly diminish, the intended and necessary responsibility of the Chief Magistrate himself." It is, Hamilton concluded, "far more safe [that] there should be a single object for the jealousy and watchfulness of the people; . . . all multiplication of the Executive is rather dangerous than friendly to liberty."

James Iredell, who played a leading role in the North Carolina ratifying convention and later became a justice of the Supreme Court, said that under the proposed Constitution the President "is of a very different nature from a monarch. He is to be . . . personally responsible for any abuse of the great trust reposed in him." In the same convention, William R. Davie, who had been a delegate in Philadelphia, explained that the "predominant principle" on which the Convention had provided for a single executive was "the more obvious responsibility of one person." When there was but one man, said Davie, "the public were never at a loss" to fix the blame.

James Wilson, in the Pennsylvania convention, described the security furnished by a single executive as one of its "very important advantages":

The executive power is better to be trusted when it has no screen. Sir, we have a responsibility in the person of our President; he cannot act improperly, and hide either his negligence or inattention; he cannot roll upon any other person the weight of his criminality; no appointment can take place without his nomination; and he is responsible for every nomination he makes . . . Add to all this, that officer is placed high, and is possessed of power far from being contemptible, yet not a *single privilege*, is annexed to his character; far from being above the laws, he is amenable to them in his private character as a citizen, and in his public character by *impeachment*.

As Wilson's statement suggests, the impeachability of the President was considered to be an important element of his responsibility.

Impeachment had been included in the proposals before the Constitutional Convention from its beginning. A specific provision, making the executive removable from office on impeachment and conviction for "mal-practice or neglect of duty," was unanimously adopted even before it was decided that the executive would be a single person."

The only major debate on the desirability of impeachment occurred when it was moved that the provision for impeachment be dropped, a motion that was defeated by a vote of eight states to two.

One of the arguments made against the impeachability of the executive was that he "would periodically be tried for his behavior by his electors" and "ought to be subject to no intermediate trial, by impeachment." Another was that the executive could "do no criminal act without Coadjutors [assistants] who may be punished. Without his subordinates, it was asserted, the executive "can do nothing of consequence," and they would "be amenable by impeachment to the public Justice."

This latter argument was made by Gouveneur Morris of Pennsylvania, who abandoned it during the course of the debate, concluding that the executive should be impeachable. Before Morris changed his position, however, George Mason had replied to his earlier argument: "Shall any man be above justice? Above all shall that man be above it, who can commit the most extensive injustice? When great crimes were committed he was for punishing the principal as well as the Coadjutors."

James Madison of Virginia argued in favor of impeachment stating that some provision was "indispensible" to defend the community against "the incapacity, negligence or perfidy of the chief Magistrate." With a single executive, Madison argued, unlike a legislature whose collective nature provided security, "loss of capacity or corruption was more within the compass of probable events, and either of them might be fatal to the Republic." Benjamin Franklin supported impeachment as "favorable to the executive"; where it was not available and the chief magistrate had "rendered himself obnoxious," recourse was had to assassination. The Constitution should provide for the "regular punishment of the Executive when his misconduct should deserve it, and for his honorable acquittal when he should be unjustly accused." Edmund Randolph also defended "the propriety of impeachments":

> The Executive will have great opportunitys of abusing his power; particularly in time of war when the military force, and in some respects the public money will be in his hands. Should no regular punishment be provided it will be irregularly inflicted by tumults & insurrections.

The one argument made by the opponents of impeachment to which no direct response was made during the debate was that the executive would be too dependent on the legislature—that, as Charles Pinckney put it, the legislature would hold impeachment "as a rod over the Executive and by that means effectually destroy his independence." That issue, which involved the forum for trying impeachments and the mode of electing the executive, troubled the Convention until its closing days. Throughout its deliberations on ways to avoid executive subservience to the legislature, however, the Convention never reconsidered its early decision to make the executive removable through the process of impeachment.

2. Adoption of "High Crimes and Misdemeanors"

Briefly, and late in the convention, the framers addressed the question how to describe the grounds for impeachment consistent with its intended function. They did so only after the mode of the President's election was settled in a way that did not make him (in the words of James Wilson) "the Minion of the Senate."

The draft of the Constitution then before the Convention provided for his removal upon impeachment and conviction for "treason or bribery." George Mason objected that these grounds were too limited:

> Why is the provision restrained to Treason & bribery only? Treason as defined in the Constitution will not reach many great and dangerous offenses. Hastings is not guilty of Treason. Attempts to subvert the Constitution may not be Treason as above defined-As bills of attainder which have saved the British Constitution are forbidden, it is the more necessary to extend: the power of impeachments.

Mason then moved to add the word "maladministration" to the other two grounds. Maladministration was a term in use in six of the thirteen state constitutions as a ground for impeachment, including Mason's home state of Virginia.

When James Madison objected that "so vague a term will be equivalent to a tenure during pleasure of the Senate," Mason withdrew "maladministration" and substituted "high crimes and misdemeanors agst. the State," which was adopted eight states to three, apparently with no further debate.

That the framers were familiar with English parliamentary impeachment proceedings is clear. The impeachment of Warren Hastings, Governor-General of India, for high crimes and misdemeanors was voted just a few weeks before the beginning of the Constitutional Convention and George Mason referred to it in the debates. Hamilton, in *Federalist* No.65, referred to Great Britain as "the model from which [impeachment] has been borrowed." Furthermore, the framers were well-educated men. Many were also lawyers. Of these, at least nine had studied law in England.

The Convention had earlier demonstrated its familiarity with the term "high misdeameanor." A draft constitution had used "high misdemeanor" in its provision for the extradition of offenders from one state to another. The Convention, apparently unanimously struck "high misdemeanor" and inserted "other crime," "in order to comprehend all proper cases: it being doubtful whether 'high misdemeanor' had not a technical meaning too limited."

The "technical meaning" referred to is the parliamentary use of the term "high misdemeanor." Blackstone's *Commentaries on the Laws of England*—a work cited by delegates in other portions of the Convention's deliberations and which Madison later described (in the Virginia ratifying convention) as "a book which is in every man's hand"—included "high misdemeanors" as one term for positive offenses "against the king and government. The "first and principal" high misdemeanor, according to Blackstone, was "mal-administration of such high officers, as are in public trust and employment," usually punished by the method of parliamentary impeachment.

"High Crimes and Misdemeanors" has traditionally been considered a "term of art," like such other constitutional phrases as "levying war" and "due process." The Supreme Court has held that such phrases must be con-strued, not according to modern usage, but according to what the framers meant when they adopted them. Chief Justice Marshall wrote of another such phrase:

> It is a technical term. It is used in a very old statute of that country whose language is our language, and whose laws form the substra-tum of our laws. It is scarcely conceivable that the term was not employed by the framers of our constitution in the sense which had been affixed to it by those from whom we borrowed it.

3. Grounds for Impeachment

Mason's suggestion to add "maladministration," Madison's objection to it as "vague," and Mason's substitution of "high crimes and misdemeanors against the State," are the only comments in the Philadelphia convention specifi-cally directed to the constitutional language describing the grounds for impeachment of the President. Mason's objection to limiting the grounds to treason and bribery was that treason would "not reach many great and dan-gerous offences" including "[a]ttempts to subvert the Constitution." His will-ingness to substitute "high Crimes and Misdemeanors," especially given his apparent familiarity with the English use of the term as evidenced by his reference to the Warren Hastings impeachment, suggests that he believed "high Crimes and Misdemeanors" would cover the offenses about which he was concerned.

Contemporaneous comments on the scope of impeachment are persuasive as to the intention of the framers. In *Federalist* No. 65, Alexander Hamilton described the subject of impeachment as "those offences which proceed from the misconduct of public men, or, in other words, from the abuse or violation of some public trust. They are of a nature which may with peculiar propriety be denominated POLITICAL, as they relate chiefly to injuries done immediately to the society itself."

Comments in the state ratifying conventions also suggest that those who adopted the Constitution viewed impeachment as a remedy for usurpation or abuse of power or serious breach of trust. Thus, Charles Cotesworth Pinckney of South Carolina stated that the impeachment power of the House reaches "those who behave amiss, or betray their public trust." Edmund Randolph said in the Virginia convention that the President may be impeached if he "misbehaves." He later cited the example of the President's receipt of presents or emoluments from a foreign power in violation of the constitutional prohibition of Article I, section 9. In the same convention George Mason argued that the President might use his pardoning power to "pardon crimes which were advised by himself" or, before indictment or conviction, "to stop inquiry and prevent detection." James Madison responded:

> [I]f the President be connected, in any suspicious manner, with any person, and there be grounds to believe he will shelter him, the House of Representatives can impeach him; they can remove him if found guilty . . .

In reply to the suggestion that the President could summon the Senators of only a few states to ratify a treaty, Madison said,

> Were the President to commit anything so atrocious . . . he would be impeached and convicted, as a majority of the states would be affected by his misdemeanor.

Edmund Randolph referred to the checks upon the President:

> It has too often happened that powers delegated for the purpose of
> promoting the happiness of a community have been perverted to the
> advancement of the personal emoluments of the agents of the peo-
> ple; but the powers of the President are too well guarded and checked
> to warrant this illiberal aspersion.

Randolph also asserted, however, that impeachment would not reach errors
of judgment: "No man ever thought of impeaching a man for an opinion. It
would be impossible to discover whether the error in opinion resulted from a
wilful mistake of the heart, or an involuntary fault of the head."

James Iredell made a similar distinction in the North Carolina convention, and on the basis of this principle said, "I suppose the only instances, in
which the President would be liable to impeachment, would be where he had
received a bribe, or had acted from some corrupt motive or other." But he
went on to argue that the President

> Must certainly be punishable for giving false information to the
> Senate. He is to regulate all intercourse with foreign powers, and it
> is his duty to impart to the Senate every material intelligence he
> receives. If it should appear that he has not given them full informa-
> tion, but has concealed important intelligence which he ought to
> have communicated, and by that means induced them to enter into
> measures injurious to their country, and which they would not have
> consented to had the true state of things been disclosed to them,—
> in this case, I ask whether, upon an impeachment for a misdemeanor
> upon such an account, the Senate would probably favor him.

In short the framers who discussed impeachment in the state ratifying conventions, as well as other delegates who favored the Constitution, implied
that it reached offenses against the government, and especially abuses of
constitutional duties. The opponents did not argue that the grounds for
impeachment had been limited to criminal offenses.

An extensive discussion of the scope of the impeachment power occurred
in the House of Representatives in the First Session of the First Congress.
The House was debating the power of the President to remove the head of an
executive department appointed by him with the advice and consent of the

Senate, an issue on which it ultimately adopted the position, urged primarily by James Madison, that the Constitution vested the power exclusively in the President. The discussion in the House lends support to the view that the framers intended the impeachment power to reach failure of the President to discharge the responsibilities of this office.

Madison argued during the debate that the president would be subject to impeachment for "the wanton removal of meritorious officers." He also contended that the power of the President unilaterally to remove subordinates was "absolutely necessary" because "it will make him in a peculiar manner, responsible for [the] conduct" of executive officers. It would, Madison said, subject him to impeachment himself, if he suffers them to perpetrate with impunity high crimes or misdemeanors against the United States, or neglects to superintend their conduct, so as to check their excesses.

Elbridge Gerry of Massachusetts, who had also been a framer though he had opposed the ratification of the Constitution, disagreed with Madison's contentions about the impeachablility of the President. He could not be impeached for dismissing a good officer, Gerry said, because he would be "doing an act which the Legislature has submitted to his discretion." And he should not be held responsible for the acts of subordinate officers, who were themselves subject to impeachment and should bear their own responsibility.

Another framer, Abraham Baldwin of Georgia, who supported Madison's position on the power to remove subordinates, spoke of the President's impeachability for failure to perform the duties of the Executive. If, said Baldwin, the President "in a fit of passion" removed" all the good officers of the Government" and the Senate were unable to choose qualified successors, the consequence would be that the President "would be obliged to do the duties himself; or, if he did not, we would impeach him, and turn him out of office, as he had done others."

Those who asserted that the President has exclusive removal power suggested that it was necessary because impeachment, as Elias Boudinot of New Jersey contended, is "intended as a punishment for a crime, and not intended as the ordinary means of re-arranging the Departments," Boudinot suggested that disability resulting from sickness or accident "would not furnish any good ground for impeachment; it could not be laid as treason or bribery, nor perhaps as a high crime or misdemeanor." Fisher Ames of Massachusetts argued for the President's removal power because "mere intention [to do a mischief] would not be cause of impeachment" and "there may be numerous causes for removal which do not amount to a crime." Later in the same speech Ames suggested that impeachment was available if an officer "misbe-haves" and for "mal-conduct."

One further piece of contemporary evidence is provided by the *Lectures on Law* delivered by James Wilson of Pennsylvania in 1790 and 1791. Wilson described impeachments in the United States as "confined to political char-acters, to political crimes and misdemeanors, and to political punishment." And, he said:

> The doctrine of impeachments is of high import in the constitutions of free states. On one hand, the most powerful magistrates should be amenable to the law: on the other hand, elevated characters should not be sacrificed merely on account of their elevation. No one should be secure while he violates the constitution and the laws: every one should be secure while he observes them.

From the comments of the framers and their contemporaries, the remarks of the delegates to the state ratifying conventions, and the removal power debate in the First Congress, it is apparent that the scope of impeachment was not viewed narrowly. It was intended to provide a check on the President through impeachment, but not to make him dependent on the unbridled will of the Congress.

Impeachment, as Justice Joseph Story wrote in his *Commentaries on the Constitution* in 1833, applies to offenses of "a political character":

> Not but that crimes of a strictly legal character fall within the scope of the power; but that it has a more enlarged operation, and reaches, what are aptly termed political offenses, growing out of personal misconduct or gross neglect, or usurpation, or habitual disregard of the public interests, various in their character, and so indefinable in their actual involutions, that it is almost impossible to provide sys-tematically for them by positive law They must be examined upon very broad and comprehensive principles of public policy and duty. They must be judged of by the habits and rules and principles of diplomacy, or departmental operations and arrangements, of parlia-mentary practice, of executive customs and negotiations of foreign as well as domestic political movements; and in short, by a great variety of circumstances, as well those which aggravate as those which extenuate or justify the offensive acts which do not properly

belong to the judicial character in the ordinary administration of justice, and are far removed from the reach of municipal jurisprudence.

. . .

III. The Criminality Issue

The phrase "high Crimes and Misdemeanors" may connote "criminality" to some. This likely is the predicate for some of the contentions that only an indictable crime can constitute impeachable conduct. Other advocates of an indictable offense requirement would establish a criminal standard of impeachable conduct because that standard is definite, can be known in advance and reflects a contemporary legal view of what conduct should be punished. A requirement of criminality would require resort to familiar criminal laws and concepts to serve as standards in the impeachment process. Furthermore, this would pose problems concerning the applicability of standards of proof and the like pertaining to the trial of crimes.

The central issue raised by these concerns is whether requiring an indictable offense is an essential element of impeachable conduct is consistent with the purposes and intent of the framers in establishing the impeachment power and in setting a constitutional standard for the exercise of that power. This issue must be considered in light of the historical evidence of the framers' intent. It is also useful to consider whether the purposes of impeachment and criminal law are such that indictable offenses can, consistent with the Constitution, be an essential element of grounds for impeachment. The impeachment of a President must occur only for reasons at least as pressing as those needs of government that give rise to the creation of criminal offenses. But this does not mean that the various elements of proof, defenses, and other substantive concepts surrounding an indictable offense control the impeachment process. Nor does it mean that state or federal criminal codes are necessarily the place to turn to provide a standard under the United States Constitution. Impeachment is a constitutional remedy. The framers intended that the impeachment language they employed should reflect the grave misconduct that so injures or abuses our constitutional institutions and form of government as to justify impeachment.

This view is support by the historical evidence of the constitutional meaning of the words "high Crimes and Misdemeanors." That evidence is set out above. It establishes that the phrase "high Crimes and Misdemeanors"—which over a period of centuries has evolved into the English standard of impeachable conduct—has a special historical meaning different from the ordinary meaning of the terms "crimes" and "misdemeanors." "High Misdemeanors" referred to a category of offenses that subverted the system of government. Since the fourteenth century the phrase "high Crimes and Misdemeanors" had been used in English impeachment cases to charge officials with a wide range of criminal and non-criminal offenses against the institutions and fundamental principles of English government.

There is evidence that the framers were aware of the special, non-criminal meaning fo the phrase "high Crimes and Misdemeanors" in the English law of impeachment. Not only did Hamilton acknowledge Great Britain as "the model from which [impeachment] has been borrowed," but George Mason referred in the debates to the impeachment of Warren Hastings, then pending before Parliament. Indeed, Mason, who proposed the phrase "high Crimes and Misdemeanors," expressly stated his intent to encompass "[a]ttempts to subvert the Constitution."

The published records of the state ratifying conventions do not reveal an intention to limit the grounds of impeachment to criminal offenses. James Iredell said in the North Carolina debates on ratification:

> . . . , the person convicted is further liable to a trial at common law, and may receive such common law punishment as belongs to a description of such offences if it be punishable by law. Likewise, George Nicholas of Virginia distinguished disqualification to hold office from conviction for criminal conduct: If [the President] deviates from his duty, he is reponsible to his constituents . . . He will be absolutely disqualified to hold any place of profit, honor, or trust, and liable to further punishment if he has committed such high crimes as are punishable at common law.

The post-convention statements of and writings of Alexander Hamilton, James Wilson, and James Madison—each a participant in the Consititutional Convention—show that they regarded impeachment as an appropriate device to deal with offenses against constitutional government by those who hold civil office, and not a device limited to criminal offenses. Hamilton, in discussing the advantages of a single rather than a plural executive, explained that a single executive gave the people "the opportunity of discovering with facility and clearness the misconduct of the person they trust, in order either to their removal from office, or to their actual punishment in cases which admit of it." Hamilton further wrote, "Man, in public trust, will much oftener act in such a manner as to render him unworthy of being any longer trusted, than in such a manner as to make him obnoxious to legal punishment."

The American experience with impeachment, which is summarized above, reflects the principle that impeachable conduct need not be criminal. Of the thirteen impeachments voted by the House since 1789, at least ten involved one or more allegations that did not charge a violation of criminal law.

Impeachment and the criminal law serve fundamentally different purposes. Impeachment is the first step in a remedial process—removal from office and possible disqualification from holding future office. The purpose of impeachment is not personal punishment; its function is primarily to maintain constitutional government. Furthermore, the Constitution itself provides that impeachment is no substitute for the ordinary process of criminal law since its specifies that impeachment does not immunize the officer from criminal liability for this wrongdoing.

The general applicability of the criminal law also makes it inappropriate as the standard for a process applicable to a highly specific situation such as removal of a President. The criminal law sets a general standard of conduct that all must follow. It does not address itself to the abuses of presidential power. In an impeachment proceeding a President is called to account for abusing powers that only a President possesses.

Other characteristics of the criminal law make criminality inappropriate as an essential element of impeachable conduct. While the failure to act may be a crime, the traditional focus of criminal law is prohibitory. Impeachable conduct, on the other hand, may include the serious failure to discharge the affirmative duties imposed on the President by the Constitution. Unlike a criminal case, the cause for the removal of a President may be based on his entire course of conduct in office. In particular situations, it may be a course of conduct more than individual acts that has a tendency to subvert constitutional government.

To confine impeachable conduct to indictable offenses may well be to set a standard so restrictive as not to reach conduct that might adversely affect the system of government. Some of the most grievous offenses against our constitutional form of government may not entail violations of the criminal law.

If criminality is to be the basic element of impeachable conduct, what is the standard of criminal conduct to be? Is it to be the criminality as known to the common law, or as divined from the Federal Criminal Code, or from an amalgam of State criminal statutes? If one is to turn to State statutes, then which of those of the States is to obtain? If the present Federal Criminal Code is to be the standard, then which of its provisions are to apply? If there is to be new Federal legislation to define the criminal standard, then presumably both the Senate and the President will take part in fixing that standard. How is this to be accomplished without encroachment upon the constitutional provision that "the sole power" of impeachment is vested in the House of Representatives?

A requirement of criminality would be incompatible with the intent of the framers to provide a mechanism broad enough to maintain the integrity of constitutional government. Impeachment is a constitutional safety valve; to fulfill this function, it must be flexible enough to cope with exigencies not now foreseeable. Congress has never undertaken to define impeachable offenses in the criminal code. Even a respecting grounds for impeachment, the federal statute establishing the criminal offense for civil officers generally was enacted over seventy-five years after the Constitutional Convention.

In sum, to limit impeachable conduct to criminal offenses would be incompatible with the evidence concerning the constitutional meaning of the phrase "high Crimes and Misdemeanors" and would frustrate the purpose that the framers intended for impeachment. State and federal criminal laws are not written in order to preserve the nation against serious abuse of the presidential office. But this is the purpose of the constitutional provision for the impeachment of a President and that purpose gives meaning to "high Crimes and Misdemeanors."

APPENDIX II

The Articles of Impeachment against
President Richard Nixon

On July 27, 1974, the House Judiciary Committee adopted the three following articles of impeachment against President Richard Nixon:

RESOLVED, That Richard M. Nixon, President of the United States, is impeached for high crimes and misdemeanours, and that the following articles of impeachment to be exhibited to the Senate:

ARTICLES OF IMPEACHMENT EXHIBITED BY THE HOUSE OF REPRESENTATIVES OF THE UNITED STATES OF AMERICA IN THE NAME OF ITSELF AND OF ALL OF THE PEOPLE OF THE UNITED STATES OF AMERICA, AGAINST RICHARD M. NIXON, PRESIDENT OF THE UNITED STATES OF AMERICA, IN MAINTENANCE AND SUPPORT OF ITS IMPEACHMENT AGAINST HIM FOR HIGH CRIMES AND MISDEMEANOURS.

ARTICLE I

In his conduct of the office of President of the United States, Richard M. Nixon, in violation of his constitutional oath faithfully to execute the office of President of the United States and, to the best of his ability, preserve, protect, and defend the Constitution of the United States, and in violation of his consitutional duty to take care that the laws be faithfully executed, has prevented, obstructed, and impeded the administration of justice, in that:

On June 17, 1972, and prior thereto, agents of the Committee for the Re-election of the President committed unlawful entry of the headquarters of the Democratic National Committee in Washington, District of Columbia, for the purpose of securing political intelligence. Subsequent thereto, Richard M. Nixon, using the powers of his high office, engaged personally and through his close subordinates and agents, in a course of conduct or plan designed to delay, impede, and obstruct the investigation of such illegal entry; to cover up, conceal and protect those responsible; and to conceal the existence and scope of other unlawful covert activities.

The means used to implement this course of conduct or plan included one or more of the following:

1. making false or misleading statements to lawfully authorized investigative officers and employees of the United States;
2. withholding relevant and material evidence or information from lawfully authorized investigative officers and employees of the United States;
3. approving, condoning, acquiescing in, and counselling witnesses with respect to the giving of false or misleading statements to lawfully authorized investigative officers and employees of the United States and false or misleading testimony in duly instituted judicial and congressional proceedings;
4. interfering or endeavouring to interfere with the conduct of investigations by the Department of Justice of the United States, the Federal Bureau of Investigation, the office of Watergate Special Prosecution Force, and Congressional Committees;
5. approving, condoning, and acquiescing in, the surreptitious payment of substantial sums of money for the purpose of obtaining the silence or influencing the testimony of witnesses, potential witnesses or individuals who participated in such unlawful entry and other illegal activities;
6. endeavouring to misuse the Central Intelligence Agency, an agency of the United States;
7. disseminating information received from officers of the Department of Justice of the United States to subjects of investigations conducted by lawfully authorized investigative officers and employees of the United States, for the purpose of aiding and assisting such subjects in their attempts to avoid criminal liability;
8. making or causing to be made false or misleading public statements for the purpose of deceiving the people of the United States into

believing that a thorough and complete investigation had been conducted with respect to allegations of misconduct on the part of personnel of the executive branch of the United States and personnel of the Committee for the Re-election of the President, and that there was no involvement of such personnel in such misconduct: or

9. endeavouring to cause prospective defendants, and individuals duly tried and convicted, to expect favoured treatment and consideration in return for their silence or false testimony, or rewarding individuals for their silence or false testimony.

In all of this, Richard M. Nixon has acted in a manner contrary to his trust as President and subversive of constitutional government, to the great prejudice of the cause of law and justice and to the manifest injury of the people of the United States.

Wherefore Richard M. Nixon, by such conduct, warrants impeachment and trial, and removal from office.

ARTICLE II

Using the powers of the office of President of the United States, Richard M. Nixon, in violation of his constitutional oath faithfully to execute the office of President of the United States and, to the best of his ability, preserve, protect, and defend the Constitution of the United States, and in disregard of his constitutional duty to take care that the laws be faithfully executed, has repeatedly engaged in conduct violating the constitutional rights of citizens, impairing the due and proper administration of justice and the conduct of lawful inquiries, or contravening the laws governing agencies of the executive branch and the purposed of these agencies.

This conduct has included one or more of the following:

1. He has, acting personally and through his subordinates and agents, endeavoured to obtain from the Internal Revenue Service, in violation of the constitutional rights of citizens, confidential information contained in income tax returns for purposed not authorized by law, and to cause, in violation of the constitutional rights of citizens, income tax audits or other income tax investigations to be initiated or conducted in a discriminatory manner.

2. He misused the Federal Bureau of Investigation, the Secret Service, and other executive personnel, in violation or disregard of the constitutional rights of citizens, by directing or authorizing such agencies or personnel to conduct or continue electronic surveillance or other investigations for purposes unrelated to national security, the enforcement of laws, or any other lawful function of his office; he did direct, authorize, or permit the use of information obtained thereby for purposes unrelated to national security, the enforcement of laws, or any other lawful function of his office; and he did direct the concealment of certain records made by the Federal Bureau of Investigation of electronic surveillance.

3. He has, acting personally and through his subordinates and agents, in violation or disregard of the constitutional rights of citizens, authorized and permitted to be maintained a secret investigative unit within the office of the President, financed in part with money derived from campaign contributions, which unlawfully utilized the resources of the Central Intelligence Agency, engaged in covert and unlawful activities, and attempted to prejudice the constitutional right of an accused to a fair trial.

4. He has failed to take care that the laws were faithfully executed by failing to act when he knew or had reason to know that his close subordinates endeavoured to impede and frustrate lawful inquiries by duly constituted executive, judicial and legislative entities concerning the unlawful entry into the headquarters of the Democratic National Committee, and the cover-up thereof, and concerning other unlawful activities including those relating to the confirmation of Richard Kleindienst as Attorney General of the United States, the electronic surveillance of private citizens, the break-in into the offices of Dr. Lewis Fielding, and the campaign financing practices of the Committee to Re-elect the President.

5. In disregard of the rule of law, he knowingly misused the executive power by interfering with agencies of the executive branch, including the Federal Bureau of Investigation, the Criminal Division, and the Office of Watergate Special Prosecution Force, of the Department of Justice, and the Central Intelligence Agency, in violation of his duty to take care that the laws be faithfully executed.

In all of this, Richard M. Nixon has acted in a manner contrary to his trust as President and subversive of constitutional government, to the great prejudice of the cause of law and justice and to the manifest injury of the people of the United States.

Wherefore Richard M. Nixon, by such conduct, warrants impeachment and trial, and removal from office.

ARTICLE III

In his conduct of the office of President of the United States, Richard M. Nixon, contrary to his oath faithfully to execute the office of President of the United States and, to the best of his ability, preserve, protect, and defend the Constitution of the United States, and in violation of his constitutional duty to take care that the laws be faithfully executed, has failed without lawful cause or excuse to produce papers and things as directed by duly authorized subpoenas issued by the Committee on the Judiciary of the House of Representatives on April 11, 1974, May 15, 1974, May 30, 1974, and June 24, 1974, and willfully disobeyed such subpoenas. The subpoenaed papers and things were deemed necessary by the Committee in order to resolve by direct evidence fundamental, factual questions relating to Presidential direction, knowledge or approval of actions demonstrated by other evidence to be substantial grounds for impeachment of the President. In refusing to produce these papers and things Richard M. Nixon, substituting his judgment as to what materials were necessary for the inquiry, interposed the powers of the Presidency against the lawful subpoenas of the House of Representatives, thereby assuming to himself functions and judgments necessary to the exercise of the sole power of impeachment vested by the Constitution in the House of Representatives.

In all of this, Richard M. Nixon has acted in a manner contrary to his trust as President and subversive of constitutional government, to the great prejudice of the cause of law and justice, and to the manifest injury of the people of the United States.

Wherefore, Richard M. Nixon, by such conduct, warrants impeachment and trial, and removal from office.

APPENDIX III

The Constitution of the United States

We the people of the United States, in Order to form a more perfect Union, establish Justice, insure domestic Tranquility, provide for the common defense, promote the general Welfare, and secure the Blessings of Liberty to ourselves and our Posterity, do ordain and establish this Constitution for the United States of America.

ARTICLE I

Section. 1. All legislative Powers herein granted shall be vested in a Congress of the United States, which shall consist of a Senate and House of Representatives.

Section. 2. The House of Representatives shall be composed of Members chosen every second Year by the People of the several States, and the Electors in each State shall have the Qualifications requisite for Electors of the most numerous Branch of the State Legislature. No Person shall be a Representative who shall not have attained to the Age of twenty five Years, and been seven Years a citizen of the United States, and who shall not, when elected, be an Inhabitant of that State in which he shall be chosen.

[Representatives and direct Taxes shall be apportioned among the several States which may be included within this Union, according to their respective Numbers, which shall be determined by adding to the whole Number of free Persons, including those bound to Service for a Term of Years, and excluding Indians not taxed, three fifths of all other Persons.] The actual Enumeration shall be made within three Years after the first Meeting of the Congress of the United States, and within every subsequent Term of ten Years, in such Manner as they shall by Law direct. The number of Representatives shall not exceed one for every thirty Thousand, but each State shall have at Least one Representative; and until such enumeration shall be made, the State of New Hampshire shall be entitled to chuse three, Massachusetts eight, Rhode Island and Providence Plantations one, Connecticut five, New York six, New Jersey four, Pennsylvania eight, Delaware one, Maryland six, Virginia ten, North Carolina five, South Carolina five, and Georgia three.

When vacancies happen in the Representation from any State, the Executive Authority thereof shall issue Writs of Election to fill such Vacancies.

The House of Representatives shall chuse their Speaker and other Officers; and shall have the sole Power of Impeachment.

Section. 3. The Senate of the United States shall be composed of two Senators from each State, [chosen by the legislature thereof,] for six Years; and each Senator shall have one Vote. Immediately after they shall be assembled in Consequence of the first Election, they shall be divided as equally as may be into three Classes. The Seats of the Senators of the first Class shall be vacated at the Expiration of the second Year, of the second Class at the Expiration of the fourth Year, and of the third Class at the expiration of the sixth Year, so that one third may be chosen every second Year; [and if vacancies happen by Resignation, or otherwise, during the Recess of the Legislature of any State, the Executive thereof may make temporary Appointments until the next Meeting of the Legislature, which shall then fill such Vacancies.]

No person shall be a Senator who shall not have attained to the Age of thirty Years, and been nine Years a Citizen of the United States, and who shall not, when elected, be an Inhabitant of that State for which he shall be chosen.

The Vice President of the United States shall be President of the Senate, but shall have no Vote, unless they be equally divided.

The Senate shall chuse their other Officers, and also a President pro tempore, in the Absence of the Vice-President, or when he shall exercise the Office of President of the United States.

The Senate shall have the sole Power to try all Impeachments. When sitting for that Purpose, they shall be on Oath or Affirmation. When the President of the United States is tried, the Chief Justice shall preside: And no Person shall be convicted without the Concurrence of two thirds of the Members present.

Judgment in Cases of Impeachment shall not extend further than to removal from Office, and disqualification to hold and enjoy any Office of honor, Trust or Profit under the United States: but the Party convicted shall nevertheless be liable and subject to Indictment, Trial, Judgment and Punishment, according to Law.

Section. 4. The Times, Places and Manner of holding Elections for Senators and Representatives, shall be prescribed in each State by the Legislature thereof; but the Congress may at any time by Law make or alter such Regulations, except as to the Places of chusing Senators.

The Congress shall assemble at least once in every Year, and such Meeting shall be [on the first Monday in December,] unless they shall by law appoint a different Day.

Section. 5. Each House shall be the Judge of the Elections, Returns and Qualifications of its own Members, and a Majority of each shall constitute a Quorum to do Business; but a smaller Number may adjourn from day to day, and may be authorized to compel the Attendance of absent Members, in such Manner, and under such Penalties as each House may provide.

Each house may determine the Rules of its Proceedings, punish its Members for disorderly Behavior, and, with the Concurrence of two-thirds, expel a Member.

Each house shall keep a Journal of its Proceedings, and from time to time publish the same, excepting such Parts as may in their Judgment require Secrecy; and the Yeas and Nays of the Members of either House on any question shall, at the Desire of one fifth of those Present, be entered on the Journal.

Neither House, during the Session of Congress, shall, without the Consent of the other, adjourn for more than three days, nor to any other Place than that in which the two Houses shall be sitting.

Section. 6. The Senators and Representatives shall receive a Compensation for their Services, to be ascertained by Law, and paid out of the Treasury of the United States. They shall in all Cases, except Treason, Felony and Breach of the Peace, be privileged from Arrest during their Attendance at the Session of their respective Houses, and in going to and returning from the same; and for any Speech or Debate in either House, they shall not be questioned in any other Place.

No Senator or Representative shall, during the Time for which he was elected, be appointed to any civil Office under the Authority of the United States, which shall have been created, or the Emoluments whereof shall have been encreased during such time; and no Person holding any Office under the United States, shall be a Member of either House during his Continuance in Office.

Section. 7. All Bills for raising Revenue shall originate in the House of Representatives; but the Senate may propose or concur with Amendments as on other Bills.

Every Bill which shall have passed the House of Representatives and the Senate, shall, before it become a Law, be presented to the President of the United States; If he approve he shall sign it, but if not he shall return it, with his Objections to that House in which it shall have originated, who shall enter the Objections at large on their Journal, and proceed to reconsider it. If after such Reconsideration two thirds of that house shall agree to pass the Bill, it shall be sent, together with the Objections, to the other House, by which it shall likewise be reconsidered, and if approved by two thirds of that House, it shall become a Law. But in all such Cases the Votes of both Houses shall be determined by yeas and Nays, and the Names of the Persons voting for and against the Bill shall be entered on the Journal of each House respectively. If any Bill shall not be returned by the President within ten Days (Sundays excepted) after it shall have been presented to him, the Same shall be a Law, in like Manner as if he had signed it, unless the Congress by their Adjournment prevent its Return, in which case it shall not be a Law.

Every Order, Resolution, or Vote to which the Concurrence of the Senate and House of Representatives may be necessary (except on a question of Adjournment) shall be presented to the President of the United States; and before the Same shall take Effect, shall be approved by him, or being disapproved by him, shall be repassed by two thirds of the Senate and House of Representatives, according to the Rules and Limitations prescribed in the Case of a Bill.

Section. 8. The Congress shall have Power To lay and collect Taxes, Duties, Imposts and Excises, to pay the Debts and provide for the common Defence and general Welfare of the United States; but all Duties, Imposts and Excises shall be uniform throughout the United States;

To borrow Money on the credit of the United States;

To regulate Commerce with foreign Nations, and among the several States, and with the Indian Tribes;

To establish an uniform Rule of Naturalization, and uniform Laws on the subject of Bankruptcies throughout the United States;

To coin Money, regulate the Value thereof, and of foreign Coin, and fix the Standard of Weights and Measures;

To provide for the Punishment of counterfeiting the Securities and current Coin of the United States;

To establish Post Offices and Post Roads;

To promote the Progress of Science and useful Arts, by securing for limited Times to Authors and Inventors the exclusive Right to their respective Writings and Discoveries;

To constitute Tribunals inferior to the supreme Court;

To define and punish Piracies and Felonies committed on the high Seas, and Offenses against the Law of Nations;

To declare War, grant Letters of Marque and Reprisal, and make Rules concerning Captures on Land and Water;

To raise and support Armies, but no Appropriation of Money to that Use shall be for a longer Term than two Years;

To provide and maintain a Navy;

To make Rules for the Government and Regulation of the land and naval Forces;

To provide for calling forth the Militia to execute the Laws of the Union, suppress Insurrections and repel Invasions;

To provide for organizing, arming, and disciplining, the Militia, and for governing such Part of them as may be employed in the Service of the United States, reserving to the States respectively, the Appointment of the Officers, and the Authority of training the Militia according to the discipline prescribed by Congress;

To exercise exclusive Legislation in all Cases whatsoever, over such District (not exceeding ten Miles square) as may, by Cession of particular States, and the Acceptance of Congress, become the Seat of the Government of the United States, and to exercise like Authority over all Places purchased by the Consent of the Legislature of the State in which the Same shall be, for the Erection of Forts, Magazines, Arsenals, dock-Yards, and other needful Buildings;—And

To make all Laws which shall be necessary and proper for carrying into Execution the foregoing Powers, and all other Powers vested by this Constitution in the Government of the United States, or in any Department or Officer thereof.

Section. 9. The Migration or Importation of such Persons as any of the States now existing shall think proper to admit, shall not be prohibited by the Congress prior to the Year one thousand eight hundred and eight, but a

Tax or Duty may be imposed on such Importation, not exceeding ten dollars for each Person.

The Privilege of the Writ of Habeas Corpus shall not be suspended, unless when in Cases of Rebellion or Invasion the public Safety may require it.

No Bill of Attainder or ex post facto Law shall be passed.

No Capitation, or other direct, Tax shall be laid, unless in Proportion to the Census or Enumeration herein before directed to be taken.

No Tax or Duty shall be laid on Articles exported from any State.

No Preference shall be given by any Regulation of Commerce or Revenue to the Ports of one State over those of another: nor shall Vessels bound to, or from, one State, be obliged to enter, clear, or pay Duties in another.

No Money shall be drawn from the Treasury, but in Consequence of Appropriations made by Law; and a regular Statement and Account of the Receipts and Expenditures of all public Money shall be published from time to time.

No Title of Nobility shall be granted by the United States: And no Person holding any Office of Profit or Trust under them, shall, without the Consent of the Congress, accept of any present, Emolument, Office, or Title, of any kind whatever, from any King, Prince, or foreign State.[1]

Section 10. No State shall enter into any Treaty, Alliance, or Confederation; grant Letters of Marque and Reprisal; coin Money; emit Bills of Credit; make any Thing but gold and silver Coin a Tender in Payment of Debts; pass any Bill of Attainder, ex post facto Law, or Law impairing the Obligation of Contracts, or grant any Title of Nobility.

No State shall, without the Consent of the Congress, lay any Imposts or Duties on Imports or Exports, except what may be absolutely necessary for executing it's inspection Laws: and the net Produce of all Duties and Imposts, laid by any State on Imports or Exports, shall be for the Use of the Treasury of the United States; and all such Laws shall be subject to the Revision and Controul of the Congress.

No State shall, without the Consent of Congress, lay any Duty of Tonnage, keep Troops, or Ships of War in time of Peace, enter into any Agreement or Compact with another State, or with a foreign Power, or engage in War, unless actually invaded, or in such imminent Danger as will not admit of delay.

---

1   Article I, Section 9: The emoluments clause, which President Trump appears to have violated. See Chapter 5.

ARTICLE II

Section. 1. The executive Power shall be vested in a President of the United States of America. He shall hold his Office during the Term of four Years, and, together with the Vice President, chosen for the same Term, be elected, as follows:

Each State shall appoint, in such Manner as the Legislature thereof may direct, a Number of Electors, equal to the whole Number of Senators and Representatives to which the State may be entitled in the Congress: but no Senator or Representative, or Person holding an Office of Trust or Profit under the United States, shall be appointed an Elector.

[The Electors shall meet in their respective States, and vote by Ballot for two Persons, of whom one at least shall not be an Inhabitant of the same State with themselves. And they shall make a List of all the Persons voted for, and of the Number of Votes for each; which List they shall sign and certify, and transmit sealed to the Seat of the Government of the United States, directed to the President of the Senate. The President of the Senate shall, in the Presence of the Senate and House of Representatives, open all the Certificates, and the Votes shall then be counted. The Person having the greatest Number of Votes shall be the President, if such Number be a Majority of the whole Number of Electors appointed; and if there be more than one who have such Majority, and have an equal Number of Votes, then the House of Representatives shall immediately chuse by Ballot one of them for President; and if no Person have a Majority, then from the five highest on the List the said House shall in like Manner chuse the President. But in chusing the President, the Votes shall be taken by States, the Representation from each State having one Vote; a quorum for this Purpose shall consist of a Member or Members from two thirds of the States, and a Majority of all the States shall be necessary to a Choice. In every Case, after the Choice of the President, the Person having the greatest Number of Votes of the Electors shall be the Vice President. But if there should remain two or more who have equal Votes, the Senate shall chuse from them by Ballot the Vice President.]

The Congress may determine the Time of chusing the Electors, and the Day on which they shall give their Votes; which Day shall be the same throughout the United States.

No Person except a natural born Citizen, or a Citizen of the United States, at the time of the Adoption of this Constitution, shall be eligible to the Office of President; neither shall any person be eligible to that Office who shall not have attained to the Age of thirty five Years, and been fourteen Years a Resident within the United States.

[In Case of the Removal of the President from Office, or of his Death, Resignation, or Inability to discharge the Powers and Duties of the said Office, the Same shall devolve on the Vice President, and the Congress may by Law provide for the Case of Removal, Death, Resignation or Inability, both of the President and Vice President, declaring what Officer shall then act as President, and such Officer shall act accordingly, until the Disability be removed, or a President shall be elected.]

The President shall, at stated Times, receive for his Services, a Compensation, which shall neither be increased nor diminished during the Period for which he shall have been elected, and he shall not receive within that Period any other Emolument from the United States, or any of them.

Before he enter on the Execution of his Office, he shall take the following Oath or Affirmation:—"I do solemnly swear (or affirm) that I will faithfully execute the Office of President of the United States, and will to the best of my Ability, preserve, protect and defend the Constitution of the United States."

Section. 2. The President shall be Commander in Chief of the Army and Navy of the United States, and of the Militia of the several States, when called into the actual Service of the United States; he may require the Opinion, in writing, of the principal Officer in each of the executive Departments, upon any Subject relating to the Duties of their respective Offices, and he shall have Power to grant Reprieves and Pardons for Offenses against the United States, except in Cases of impeachment.

He shall have Power, by and with the Advice and Consent of the Senate, to make Treaties, provided two thirds of the Senators present concur; and he shall nominate, and by and with the Advice and Consent of the Senate, shall appoint Ambassadors, other public Ministers and Consuls, Judges of the supreme Court, and all other Officers of the United States, whose Appointments are not herein otherwise provided for, and which shall be established by Law: but the Congress may by Law vest the Appointment of such inferior Officers, as they think proper, in the President alone, in the Courts of Law, or in the Heads of Departments.

The President shall have Power to fill up all Vacancies that may happen during the Recess of the Senate, by granting Commissions which shall expire at the End of their next session.

Section. 3. He shall from time to time give to the Congress Information of the State of the Union, and recommend to their Consideration such Measures as he shall judge necessary and expedient; he may, on extraordinary Occasions, convene both Houses, or either of them, and in Case of Disagreement between them, with Respect to the Time of Adjournment, he may adjourn them to such Time as he shall think proper; he shall receive Ambassadors and other public Ministers; *he shall take Care that the Laws be faithfully executed,* and shall Commission all the Officers of the United States.[2]

Section 4. The President, Vice President and all civil Officers of the United States, shall be removed from Office on Impeachment for, and Conviction of, Treason, Bribery, or other high Crimes and Misdemeanors.[3]

ARTICLE III

Section 1. The judicial Power of the United States, shall be vested in one supreme Court, and in such inferior Courts as the Congress may from time to time ordain and establish. The Judges, both of the supreme and inferior Courts, shall hold their Offices during good Behaviour, and shall, at stated Times, receive for their Services, a Compensation, which shall not be diminished during their Continuance in Office.

Section. 2. The judicial Power shall extend to all Cases, in Law and Equity, arising under this Constitution, the Laws of the United States, and Treaties made, or which shall be made, under their Authority;—to all Cases affecting Ambassadors, other public Ministers and Consuls;—to all Cases of admiralty and maritime Jurisdiction;—to Controversies to which the United States shall be a Party;—to Controversies between two or more States;—[between a State and Citizens of another State;—] between Citizens of different States;—between Citizens of the same State claiming Lands under Grants of different States, and [between a State, or the Citizens thereof, and foreign States, Citizens or Subjects.]

---

2   Article II, Section 3: Constitutional duties of the president, including to "take Care that the Laws be faithfully executed." Emphasis is my own.

In his refusal to protect the integrity of US elections against Russian cyberattack and alleged attempts to impede the Russia investigation, President Trump is refusing to fulfill his constitutional duty as president. See Chapter 3.

3   Article II, Section 4: Disqualification—the acts for which a sitting president may be impeached. See Chapter 2.

In all cases affecting Ambassadors, other public Ministers and Consuls, and those in which a State shall be Party, the supreme Court shall have original Jurisdiction. In all the other Cases before mentioned, the supreme Court shall have appellate Jurisdiction, both as to Law and Fact, with such Exceptions, and under such Regulations as the Congress shall make.

The Trial of all Crimes, except in Cases of Impeachment, shall be by Jury; and such Trial shall be held in the State where the said Crimes shall have been committed; but when not committed within any State, the Trial shall be at such Place or Places as the Congress may by Law have directed.

Section. 3. Treason against the United States, shall consist only in levying War against them, or in adhering to their Enemies, giving them Aid and Comfort. No Person shall be convicted of Treason unless on the Testimony of two Witnesses to the same overt Act, or on Confession in open Court.[4]

The Congress shall have power to declare the punishment of Treason, but no Attainder of Treason shall work Corruption of Blood, or Forfeiture except during the Life of the Person attainted.

---

4   Article III, Section 3: The definition of treason. While President Trump may have committed treason in colluding with Russia to get elected, I do not believe there is sufficient evidence to warrant impeachment for this charge at this time. See Chapter 6.

Selected Sources

Berger, Raoul. *Impeachment: The Constitutional Problems.* Cambridge, MA: Harvard University Press, 1973.

Black, Charles L., Jr. *Impeachment: A Handbook.* New Haven: Yale University Press, 1974.

Dershowitz, Alan. *The Case Against Impeaching Trump.* New York: Hot Books, 2018.

Farrand, Max (ed.). *The Records of the Federal Convention of 1787.* New Haven: Yale University Press, 1966.

Farrell, John A. *Richard Nixon: The Life.* New York: Doubleday, 2017.

Gerhardt, Michael J. *The Federal Impeachment Process: A Constitutional and Historical Analysis.* Chicago: The University of Chicago Press, 2000.

Hearings of the Committee on the Judiciary, House of Representatives, 93rd Congress, 2nd Session. *Debate on Articles of Impeachment.* Washington, DC: US Government Printing Office, 1974.

Holtzman, Elizabeth with Cooper, Cynthia L. *The Impeachment of George W. Bush: A Practical Guide for Concerned Citizens.* New York: Nation Books, 2006.

The Final Report of the Committee on the Judiciary, House of Representatives. *Impeachment of Richard M. Nixon, President of the United States.* New York: Bantam Books, 1975.

Isikoff, Michael and David Corn. *Russian Roulette: The Inside Story of Putin's War on America and the Election of Donald Trump.* New York: Hachette Book Group, 2018.

Kutler, Stanley J. *The Wars of Watergate.* New York: W.W. Norton, 1992.

Lichtman, Allan J. The Case for Impeachment. New York: Dey Street Books, 2017.

Teachout, Zephyr. *Corruption in America: From Ben Franklin's Snuff Box to Citizen's United.* Cambridge, MA: Harvard University Press, 2014.

Tribe, Laurence, and Joshua Matz. *To End a Presidency: The Power of Impeachment.* New York: Basic Books, 2018.

Sunstein, Cass R. *Impeachment: A Citizen's Guide.* Cambridge, MA: Harvard University Press, 2017.

Newspapers, Periodicals, and other Outlets Cited

Axios (Arlington, VA)
Bloomberg News (New York, NY)
CBS (New York, NY)
CNN (New York, NY)
Foreign Policy (Washington, DC)
Forbes (New York, NY)
Fox (New York, NY)
The Guardian (Kings Place, London)
Huffington Post (New York, NY)
The Intercept (New York, NY)
The Nation (New York, NY)
New York Daily News (New York, NY)
The New York Times (New York, NY)
Newsweek (New York, NY)
Politico (Arlington, VA)
TIME (New York, NY)
USA Today (McLean, VA)
Wall Street Journal (New York, NY)
The Washington Post (Washington, DC)
Wired (San Francisco, CA)